HARMONY AND MONEY

Seven Steps to Build Wealth and Marriage Two-gether

Franky Fernandes

Dedication

To all the young families with whom I've shared countless hours, listening to your unique struggles and challenges. You've given me invaluable insights, and this book is for you

Contents

INTRODUCTION

It was a typical afternoon in August 2012. The cool monsoon weather outside contrasted with the chill of the office air conditioning. As I worked, a meeting invite popped up on my screen—one I had been anticipating. I quickly locked my computer and headed to the meeting. Upon entering the room, my colleague greeted me with a smile, introduced me to a financial advisor, and we exchanged pleasantries. I had no idea that the next 45 minutes would change my financial life forever. Little did I know, this moment would reshape not only my financial future and understanding of marriage and wealth but also impact numerous others whom I would teach and coach. In fact, even this book would not have taken its current shape without that meeting.

Eye-Opener Meeting

We were doing well in our marriage, and I even wrote articles and counselled young families on relationships. Professionally, my career was thriving, and I felt I had achieved much of what I wanted. I thought my personal finances were in good shape too—but I was mistaken. Like many, I assumed that earning a good salary meant I was financially secure.

This false sense of security misled me for years, as I later discovered I wasn't as financially prepared as I thought.

Thirty minutes into the meeting, I realised I had made some serious financial mistakes. The advisor used an Excel sheet to calculate my goals and target savings, and it hit me—I wasn't saving or investing enough. The gap was alarming, and my savings were insufficient. Mentally, I tried to dismiss the reality, thinking, "I'll make up for it later." But I didn't know how. Now, I see many young families experience the same uncertainty during financial planning.

I had to rethink my budget and savings and instil a discipline that was missing. I needed to surrender unnecessary policies, buy the right insurances, and repay my home loan. It was a complete overhaul of my personal finances. I had believed I knew a lot, but now I had to do things differently. The advisor shared an investment plan, adjusted my asset allocation, and strongly encouraged me to begin a mutual fund SIP (Systematic Investment Plan).

Decisions and transformations

I wasn't fully prepared for such a significant financial change, and my wife felt the same. We both thought our situation wasn't bad, so why worry? Still, we prayerfully decided to start SIPs in mutual funds. My wife's support made it easier, and the decision-making became seamless. Looking back, I can confidently say it was the best decision we made—it transformed our financial future.

In the following days and weeks, the changes began to take effect. Regular debits from our bank accounts and the restrictions that followed became noticeable. Frequent text notifications reminded us that funds were needed in the bank, so we couldn't spend freely. This shift profoundly impacted our spending habits, making us more mindful of our finances.

Growing wealth and career

In one year, I significantly increased my savings and investments. The BSE Sensex rose by 135% from 2012 to March 2020, just before the lockdown. Although the markets fell in March 2020, they steadily grew until October 2024 as of this writing—a rise of over 100%. Overall, from 2012 to 2024, my mutual funds portfolio yielded annualised returns of 18%. Prior to 2012, I had been investing in mutual funds since 1998 but was always trying to time the market, opting for lump-sum investments and frequent trading.

My wealth grew quietly, as I wasn't actively monitoring my investments. Instead, I focused on my career. The year 2012 marked a turning point: I transitioned from mutual fund operations to IT support and eventually moved on to lead an international reporting team for over 30 countries. By 2017, I was promoted to Director of Analytics after expanding the team.

While I was advancing my career and pursuing an 18-month analytics course at ISB (Indian School of Business), my investments continued to grow silently. I improved my financial literacy during this time, but my investment strategy remained passive. Occasionally checking my portfolio left me amazed at its growth. What began as a disciplined approach transformed into a natural habit. Reflecting on this journey, I realise that my decision to invest consistently was indeed one of the best I ever made.

Embarking on the Freelance Journey

I quit my job and the corporate world in December 2020. Since 2021, I have been working as a freelance consultant, focusing on personal finance and relationship coaching. I became certified as an executive coach from CFI in 2021 and added certifications as a premarital counsellor and marriage coach in 2022. In 2023, I achieved the designation of CERTIFIED FINANCIAL PLANNER™ (CFP®) and became a mutual fund distributor. My primary goal is to assist young families in financial planning and guide them in investing in mutual funds. I encourage systematic investment plans (SIPs), knowing that this small discipline can lead to significant financial growth over time.

In the past few years, I have trained several thousand singles and families through Zoom and live sessions. My training covers essential topics such as spending, saving, charitable giving, long-term investing, and risk planning. Over the last 18 months, I have had the opportunity to coach around 80 families, helping them articulate and achieve their financial goals. Each family is unique, with distinct functioning styles, personalities, and relationship dynamics. However, I've observed some common themes: many families are in debt, borrowing has become commonplace, and most lack knowledge about equity investments and mutual funds, which I believe is the engine for growing wealth. Additionally, while many families have traditional insurance policies, few possess adequate term insurance, reflecting financial situations as chaotic as my own years ago.

As a marriage coach, I approach financial advising with a distinct perspective. I emphasise the importance of both partners participating in one-on-one financial coaching sessions. In my experience, I've noted varying marital dynamics; some couples manage their finances separately, while others show a lack of engagement from one partner. For instance, one husband insisted on proceeding without his wife, stating she wasn't knowledgeable about finances. Yet, during our session, she ended up asking insightful questions, showcasing her potential for involvement. This is my conclusion after talking and training so many families: couples who work together as a team show much more promise for growing both their wealth and their relationship.

What's in This Book?

This brings us to the essence of my book, which begins with a wedding scene. This momentous occasion often lacks an understanding of its profound significance, leading to ongoing financial conflicts in many families. I aim to merge the concepts of marriage and wealth, emphasising that both are crucial for a fulfilling life. Achieving financial stability while lacking emotional connection can lead to toxic relationships, just as a loving partnership without sufficient wealth can result in stress during retirement.

To create a fulfilling life, it's important to grow both your wealth and strengthen your marriage together. In this book, I share seven steps to help you develop both areas. I hope you and your partner will dive into this material. It's not just about making money or improving your relationship—it's about bringing both together in a smart way.

Thank you for purchasing and committing to reading this book. I hope you find it meaningful, enriching, and productive. I encourage you both to read it, discuss the questions posed, take notes, and make decisions. Six months or a year later, revisit the book to assess your progress with the seven steps. I look forward to hearing your thoughts on this journey.

Wishing you abundant love and strength as you embark on this journey together.

STEP 1 – JOINING: "COMBINE YOUR FINANCES"

Step of Commitment and Togetherness

This section includes one chapter and covers the power of unity in marriage and finances, illustrating how two individuals merge their lives, finances, and goals to become one. Through personal examples and research, it shows how joint finances strengthen trust, transparency, and shared commitment, while separate finances often lead to disconnection and conflict. This unity foundation promotes both wealth and relational health.

Chapter 1
Two Purses Become One

"In marriage, the two become one, and a strong foundation is built on this unity. No wonder, the foundation weakens when the two remain separate."

This was early 2001. She was dressed entirely in white, and I saw her walking slowly toward me. I looked at her, captivated by her lovely smile, and she gazed at me with her beautiful, sparkling eyes. We exchanged smiles as she came close and stood beside me. We faced the podium, with hundreds of guests staring at us.

On that day, I told her, "I take you to be my lawfully wedded wife, to have and to hold from this day forward, for better or for worse, for richer or poorer, in sickness and in health, to love and to cherish, until death do us part." We became husband and wife. I understood very little that day, but today, after 23 years of marriage, it makes a lot of sense.

'Until death do us part' signifies that we became one at that moment. It was a solemn occasion, marking a significant change.

This is not just a formality; it is an expression of what marriage truly is. It's a union of two individuals embarking on the journey of becoming one. A new mathematical equation is established: $1 + 1 = 1$. No doubt, it's poor math, but who cares as long as it results in a good marriage that touches every area of our lives, including finances.

My wife and I are poles apart when it comes to personality. She is an extrovert, and I am an introvert. She is from Venus, and I am from Mars—I hope you get the point. She grew up in Chennai, a metropolitan city in India, while I grew up in Mumbai. She was younger of the two girls, and I was the eldest of four brothers. I was raised by my aunt (as my parents were working in a foreign country) who never had the opportunity to complete her schooling, while my wife grew up with educated parents.

We had very different upbringings. We shared only a few commonalities: we are both Christians and fluent in English and Hindi. By personality and temperament, we haven't changed much. Yet in marriage, we decided to adopt a common outlook, common goals, and shared purposes. We resolved to move in the same direction. Prior to marriage, we thought as one person; now we think as a team. Thus, marriage is a unique relationship unlike any other. What happens in marriage doesn't occur in any other relationship.

One to Two

Just as in our daily choices, our finances were no different—everything had to reflect this new 'oneness.' Before marriage, I would buy groceries for myself, choosing only what I liked. However, soon after we got married, when I went to the supermarket, I found myself unconsciously thinking, "What does she like?" "Does she prefer this snack or that sweet?" Has that happened to you? I'm sure it has.

This step is a simple example of how my thinking changed. The same applies to my wife. She would cook everything I liked. I was blessed with dishes I hardly ate in my own home. I was lavished with many delicacies. This is a sign of partnership and togetherness. The best part is we both do it with joy. I never felt bad about making purchases for my wife, even though I was the only one working during our early marriage. This was because I had strong feelings for her, and I loved her.

This principle extends beyond purchases; it encompasses everything. The gifts we received in marriage—who do they belong to? Obviously, they belong to us both. Everything in our home—the dining table, the bed, the sofa, the chairs, the kitchen, the utensils—belongs to us both. Isn't it a unique relationship? Two individuals, different genders, different upbringings, cultures, and mannerisms come together, and the entire dynamic changes.

Two incomes or one?

If everything belongs to both of us, shouldn't the money we both earn belong to us both? Why not? Today, we both work, and our income gets credited to our respective bank accounts. The source is different, and each of us has earned it using our own abilities and skills, but the question now is, "Who does the money belong to?" The answer is simple: it belongs to both of us because we are one. The foundation in marriage is built on unity. Regardless of who contributed more or less, it now belongs to both equally. This is the far-reaching impact of this relationship called marriage. Even when my wife wasn't working and her calling was to be a homemaker, the money belonged to us both equally. This is the principle of marriage: the two become one!

Joint Managers

This applies to everyone who is married. Have you ever thought about it this way? I know it's not easy; this transition takes time, but for a healthy marriage, it will be inevitable. You both are now co-owners and co-managers of everything you brought into the marriage and everything you continue to bring. It is no longer 'my money' and 'your money.' It is 'our money.'

There is no better way to establish this co-ownership over money than by having a joint bank account where the money is pooled. You can then use this pooled account for paying bills, buying groceries, saving, and charitable giving.

Money is a powerful tool with significant implications for how we perceive and feel about it. Pooling money is more about what you think of marriage and less about the money itself. Joint bank accounts seem simple and logical for marriage, yet many couples find it difficult to implement. How is it for you both?

Research findings on joint accounts

As a marriage coach, I recommend joint accounts, recognising the impact they have on marriage. I view this as a natural step for two individuals becoming one in marriage. But is there any substance to this approach? The truth is that numerous studies have shown that joint accounts keep a happier and healthier marriage.

Jenny G. Olson from Indiana University, Scott Rick of the University of Michigan, and Deborah Small of Yale University collaborated on research that surveyed both newlyweds and couples married for over 15 years regarding the effects of combining finances versus keeping them separate. This research was conducted in March 2023. They found that couples who combined their finances were significantly happier than those who maintained separate accounts. For those who joined their finances, satisfaction in their marriages was maintained and did not decline over the first two years.

Olson also mentions that this benefit in marriage is not just a momentary effect of pooling money; it's a trend that continues over the first two years of marriage. She states, "Couples do seem to be happier when they have a joint account, at least for those first two years of marriage—and possibly later, too."

These are not isolated surveys or studies; numerous studies indicate that joint accounts are the best way for married couples to manage money, which can also strengthen their marriage.

Benefits of combining finances

According to financial expert Dave Ramsey, who hosts a TV program and YouTube channel, the benefit of combining finances is that it gives couples a much higher chance of building wealth. Specifically, he references a study of millionaires conducted by his research team.

According to an article in 'The Ascent—a Motley Fool service,' Dave Ramsey believes sharing finances is an important part of sharing a life. This is what the article states.

"Ramsey strongly recommends that couples merge their finances because he believes it fosters a shared life. The article states, "How people spend their money reflects their values, dreams, fears, and their most cherished goals. When you combine finances with your spouse, Ramsey says, 'It forces you to set goals together instead of having independent goals. Marriages are either growing together or growing apart.' You're working together as one unit instead of living as two separate people—or as roommates, as Ramsey often says. For couples who don't do this, he warns there will be less communication and a much higher probability of marital problems and divorce."

It is clear that combining finances not only helps build wealth but also strengthens the marriage relationship.

I often pose this question in my seminars on money and marriage:

"What is more important: a good marriage or sufficient wealth when you retire?"

What is your answer to this question? My answer is both. You cannot have one without the other; life will be less than fulfilling. A good marriage without money will lead to stress and many challenges. Great wealth without a good marriage will result in a miserable and toxic life.

Resistance among couples

Once, while discussing joint accounts and combining finances in a restaurant after dinner with a few people I had just met for a business meeting, one of them said,

"What if the couple separates? Aren't they risking their hard-earned money?"

I am sure such fears and insecurities prevent many couples from combining their finances. It's akin to telling a property builder, "Aren't you risking a lot of money by building a strong foundation for this building? What if it comes crashing down?" The answer is simple: on the contrary, by not building a strong foundation, the building is more likely to collapse. The same applies to marriage.

Marriage should start with trust in each other. That's the foundation. You take the initiative to trust your spouse when you give yourself completely, including the most precious possessions. That is the commitment to marriage. If you cannot commit, why did you marry?

Gina Grippo-Martinez, a wealth advisor at ALINE Wealth in the New York City area, states, "Foremost, it is a sign of unity, commitment, and trust in your relationship and your partner. You are giving each other complete access and control over your money. That is a huge commitment."

Anything you are committed to will lead to progress and eventual success. Consider your career or profession. Can you start on shaky ground, wondering if it will succeed? With that mindset, you will never succeed. Conversely, those who are committed to their jobs are the ones who grow. Is marriage not far more important than your job?

Consequences of Separate Finances

While combining finances can strengthen your marriage and increase the odds of success in wealth building, the opposite is also true. The same research mentioned earlier showed that couples who maintained completely separate accounts and those left to their own devices experienced significant declines in relationship quality over time. Finkel, one of the researchers on the team, says,

"The effect was even bigger than I anticipated; most every study shows that satisfaction declines after the wedding day."

This is what he mentions about those who had separate accounts.

Tushar and Sakshi decided to keep their bank accounts separate right from the beginning of their marriage. They also decided who would pay for what. Tushar would cover all the bills with his money, including rent and electricity bills, while Sakshi would buy groceries and other food items for the home. They attempted to balance their spending so that both took equal responsibility. One year down the line, they started having conflicts in their marriage, with money being at the top of the list.

Not having joint accounts inevitably leads to managing money separately. Managing money separately provides a sense of freedom and control for each spouse, but it also fosters a lack of transparency, resulting in weakened ties in the marriage. A couple can grow their wealth this way but will struggle to strengthen their marriage, as they often prioritise their own preferences and keep their finances secret.

A strong marriage has no secrets; everything should be open between the two.

Putting into practice

You might be thinking, "It's easier said than done." But you should make a beginning. It all starts in your thoughts. If you decide to give this a try, it will happen. While we are discussing one bank account—a joint account where money is combined—it is also perfectly acceptable and, in fact, a necessity to have individual accounts for each of you.

For example, you can retain your salary account as a single-holder account and create a new account for pooling your money. To start, set aside some money in your individual bank accounts and transfer the rest into this joint account. Decide in advance how much you will keep in your respective accounts, allowing each of you the flexibility to spend as you wish without drawing from the main joint account. Naturally, this money should be a small percentage of your salary.

The main joint account should be used for making bill payments, groceries, rent, petrol, etc., and all investments should be made from this account. This way, you both have transparency in this account, which will also help you track your expenses after budgeting. We will address budgeting separately in a later chapter.

When we first got married, I was the only working person, so I converted my salary account into a joint account, and it remains a joint account to this day. We have found it easy to manage money using this joint account and have enjoyed the benefits of operating this way even two decades later. We have grown in trust and transparency. Although I manage most of the finances, my wife has complete trust in me.

***

Long-Term Gains

Combining finances can be a game changer in marriage, enhancing the relationship more than you can imagine. Marriage is a sacred relationship, and taking the right decisions can change its trajectory. Combining money and having a joint account is one of those crucial decisions. This is truly your first step toward building your wealth and marriage together. This step may be the hardest for you, but it will also be among the most significant.

*"Combining finances is the
first step to building wealth
and marriage together."*

Questions for Discussion:
1. How can you take the first step toward a joint account today?

2. Write down your apprehensions and worries about operating a joint account.

3. What commitment do you both want to make to each other regarding combined finances?

***

Nabeel had just married at 28 years old and was eager to start his new life on the right foot. He wanted to learn how to manage money effectively but was also keen to avoid any financial conflicts with his wife. To get some guidance, he took time off to visit his trusted financial advisor. What he heard next nearly shocked him.

"What?" Nabeel leaned forward, confused. "Why a joint account? Can't we have separate accounts?"

"You can," the advisor explained. "But all your monthly bills, groceries, rent, savings, and other expenses should go from the joint account."

"So you're saying, for all practical purposes, the joint account should be our main account?" Nabeel asked, still processing the idea.

"Exactly," the advisor nodded. "Trust me, that's one of the secrets to a happy marriage and growing your wealth together. If you don't take this first step, you can't move on to the second, which is just as important."

Curiosity sparked in Nabeel's eyes. "What's the second step?" he asked.

The advisor removed his reading glasses, holding them in his right hand, and with a smile asked, "Do you know why I can see clearly with these glasses?"

Nabeel understood instantly and smiled back.

STEP 2– TALKING: "COMMUNICATE AND BE TRANSPARENT"

Step of Trust and Courage

This section includes one chapter and emphasises communication as a cornerstone of a successful marriage, especially in financial matters. Transparency, trust, and teamwork are essential to achieving harmony and financial stability. Couples who regularly communicate about finances can build wealth and resolve money conflicts, fostering a stronger bond. Without communication, misunderstandings, secrecy, and conflicts arise, damaging relationship

Chapter 2
Talking Not Hiding

"Communication is one of the pillars of a strong marriage, without which the foundations are shaky. Communication provides an opportunity for transparency regarding finances."

W ay back in 2002, the US-based company I was working for planned to close its operations in India. We were barely two years into our marriage. I made an important career move from mutual fund operations in an asset management company to an IT company as a business analyst. For the first time in my career, I was working closely with computer programmers based in Hyderabad, India, and Florida, USA. They had very little knowledge of the stock markets and mutual funds, and I was the expert who would help them code software for a mutual fund company.

Most of my day was spent training and sharing knowledge about the intricacies of mutual funds, how investors benefit from fund managers, and what features are required in the software to serve our customers. Since our team was spread across continents, I wrote numerous emails—something I had not done much before. My boss, who was based in the US, often said, "Communicate, communicate... "Overcommunication is better than undercommunication."

Just imagine if I failed to communicate the complete truth to my project team; what would be the consequences? What if I only shared bits and pieces as I felt like it? What would be the fate of the project? If I had said, "I can't share everything with you," it would have resulted in a substandard project that would not serve our customers. Communication and transparency were the foundations of my team's success and my own.

Teamwork

Building wealth is one of the significant projects a couple undertakes in marriage, just like a team. Most couples enter marriage with little knowledge of finances. However, as long as they commit to working as a team, the success of the project is guaranteed. When a couple gets married, consciously or unconsciously, whether voluntarily or involuntarily, they are part of this project. Many couples don't think of it this way; that's why problems arise. Building wealth and managing money as a team is essential for success. Knowledge is acquired along the way, and the goal is to build wealth and achieve financial freedom, which has several benefits, some of which we will discuss later in the book.

First Step

Early in our marriage, my wife and I had an argument about using credit cards.

"No, I won't use the card. I don't think we should use credit cards; it's wrong," my wife said when she realised I was using one.

I had been accustomed to using a card before marriage. Although I never used it frequently, I found it handy. My wife, on the other hand, couldn't grasp the idea that a credit card could be used without harming our finances. We talked extensively. I had to patiently explain the benefits, as she was worried. She had heard stories of financial disasters caused by credit cards. I could have discreetly used the card since I was managing our finances, but that would have been financial infidelity.

Communication, therefore, is a crucial step and key to making this project successful. Sadly, many couples don't communicate for various reasons, and those who do often don't do it effectively or with the right motives.

Essential, Not Optional

Just like in a project at work or in the community, discussing money is essential. Anyone who thinks it's optional is under an illusion. A couple cannot think, "If I don't talk about money, everything will eventually be fine because we are married and are one." That's a misunderstanding or a myth. Talking about money is as important as discussing future plans for children, their schooling, vacations, or buying a house.

Not discussing money for extended periods can create a big chasm between couples and become a stumbling block.

Not only does money management become more challenging, but building the relationship also becomes difficult. All this eventually leads to a subpar marriage and poor financial management.

Habit of Talking

Although communication is one of the most important disciplines in marriage, many couples struggle to find time, especially couples with stressful jobs. You might be thinking, "Where do we begin talking about money?" "It's so stressful to talk about money because we argue whenever we do."

The best way to succeed in communicating about money is to develop the habit of discussing other aspects of life. For example, you both can have a scheduled time to talk every day, perhaps during a walk or over coffee. Keep it deliberate so that you are compelled to communicate. Discuss what happened during the day at work or home, who you met, or what is bothering each of you.

As you grow in this habit, you will inevitably talk about money. Money is a significant part of any marriage, and it's impossible not to discuss it. We make money decisions frequently, and if you have learnt to communicate effectively, success is inevitable.

Communication Levels

Bruce and Carol Britten, in their book 'Answers to Marriage,' discuss three levels of communication in marriage.

This is something we do daily without exception. For example, "How are you?" "What did you buy today?" "I met my friend at the supermarket." "Did you see my socks?" That is level one communication.

Have you ever made decisions about which TV to buy? If you should buy a new car or a second-hand one? Should you buy a 165-litre fridge or a 200-litre one? That's level two communication.

Level three communication occurs when you discuss feelings. For example, when you share how you felt about certain purchases your spouse made or how you feel about the loan you took and its negative impact on you.

Ample opportunities to talk

Everyone does three things with their money after earning it: they spend, save, or invest and give to charity. Normally, all couples discuss these topics to varying degrees. For example, planning what to spend is budgeting. Most couples I've spoken with don't have a budget, so they miss an opportunity to talk. Discussing the budget is an excellent opportunity for couples to spend meaningful time together. Major spending or out-of-budget spending can also serve as a good opportunity to talk.

Deciding to save or invest for your financial goals is an important part of money discussions because it concerns the future. Often, both spouses don't have the same level of knowledge. Most of the time, it's the husband who knows more and handles investments, often without the wife's knowledge. The wife, on the other hand, may assume that since she doesn't know, she need not ask. In many homes, husbands have made investment decisions without discussion, jeopardising family finances.

It is therefore crucial for husbands and wives to discuss their future financial goals and invest accordingly. Despite having limited knowledge, a prudent wife's questions can prevent financial disaster.

Transparency and support go hand in hand

My wife is a speech therapist, a paramedical professional with little connection to finances. During her college years, aside from going to the bank to withdraw cash and pay fees or buy food, she had little involvement with money. However, she has offered valuable advice many times throughout our marriage, saving us from future heartaches.

Once, when we had been married for just 10 years, we planned an educational trip combined with a family vacation. I registered myself, booked train tickets, and made other arrangements. A couple of weeks before the trip, she asked me,

"Are we doing the right thing by going?

We will be spending a significant amount; won't it affect our monthly expenses? We have school fees and other expenses coming up."

I quickly checked our expenses for the month and realised we would face challenges with upcoming costs. I quickly cancelled the train tickets and the registration, profusely thanking my wife for her wise and timely counsel. So, don't underestimate the value the other spouse can bring.

Keep Each Other Informed

I remember when I got my first job in 1992 at a small proprietary firm. My salary was Rs. 1200, and I informed my aunt, with whom I was living at the time. I couldn't immediately inform my parents because they lived in southern India, and back then, we didn't even have a landline. Later, in 1993, I got my first break in the mutual fund industry with SBI Mutual Fund, and my salary quadrupled. I informed my family about my salary but never went beyond that. I never shared what I did with my money, nor did they ask me. I'm sure this is the case for most of us.

So why didn't I ever bother to tell them? Let's uncover the underlying reason why we don't inform anyone. It's simple; we think, "It's my money, and why should I tell anyone what I do with it?" Have you ever felt that way?

After marriage, two people under the same roof often think the same way. Essentially, they are saying, "It's my money, and I don't have to account for it to anyone." That's incorrect, and let me explain why.

Marriage is a unique relationship designed by our Creator. Coming from a Christian faith, my understanding is rooted in the Bible. The Bible states clearly, "The two shall become one." In other words, when you get married, a new mathematical formula is generated: one plus one equals one.

When you get married, an invisible force creates oneness. The physical union that occurs during marriage permeates every other area of your life, including money, children, and life goals. In a family of four, including two daughters, the husband cannot say, "This is my daughter, and that is her daughter." Both daughters belong equally to their parents. Likewise, the money we possess is 'ours,' not 'my money' and 'your money,' regardless of who brings in more money to the family kitty.

Therefore, it is only fair that you share openly with your spouse where you spent the money. At the start of the month, if you have budgeted and spent according to that budget, sharing this information may seem redundant. However, the value of sharing arises when either spouse spends outside the budget, especially if it involves a significant sum.

You may be wondering, "Should I share every single penny I spend, even if it is insignificant?" This is something each couple must agree upon regarding what is significant. For some, a significant sum could be Rs. 500, while for others, it might be Rs. 5000. If you agree to discuss or share any expenses that exceed this threshold, it establishes good discipline. This practice helps keep each other in check. As you develop the habit of budgeting and tracking your expenses (which we will discuss later in a subsequent chapter), sharing becomes inevitable. Such transparency will not only keep your spending in check but also strengthen your marriage.

No Secrets

According to a survey conducted by the online insurance marketplace www.policygenius.com 13% of married couples have a secret checking account, 12% have a secret savings account, 12% possess a secret credit card, 9% have a secret retirement account, 7% maintain a secret life insurance policy, and 6% have a secret will. This is known as financial infidelity. Financial infidelity encompasses any kind of deception or secrecy regarding money or spending within a relationship. Such financial secrets can undermine a marriage in the long run.

Charles never realised that his wife Sarah was a spendthrift who struggled to control her spending. Her greatest weakness was her credit card; she would swipe it thoughtlessly in any store. As a result, Charles often found himself spending excessively in some months, especially since Sarah was a homemaker. Frustrated with this lifestyle, he eventually decided to separate from her.

In contrast, Mahesh would use his credit card each month to make purchases without his wife Hema's knowledge, paying the bill at the end of the month. Both of these examples illustrate financial infidelity. Such infidelity can stem from financial decisions made before marriage as well.

Aarav took out a loan to finance his wedding and never mentioned it to his wife, Aastha. Much later in their marriage, Aarav once mentioned this loan to Aastha, leaving her heartbroken. They had a significant argument because she felt betrayed by his secrecy.

The key to preventing such secretive financial behaviours is communication. Prioritise open dialogue. Aarav believed it was acceptable not to disclose a decision made before marriage. Mahesh, on the other hand, intentionally avoided transparency to maintain control. Sarah assumed her husband would eventually know. In all these instances, communication is absent.

Make a commitment to communicate with each other and to never keep secrets. Keeping secrets undermines the very foundation of marriage, which is built on trust. Any form of infidelity can harm the marriage.

Resolving Money Conflicts

A study conducted by the American Institute of CPAs in 2021 revealed that 73% of married Americans consider financial decision-making an ongoing source of conflict in their relationships. Conflicts are inevitable in marriage, and money conflicts are no exception. Like any other conflict, the best way to handle them is through discussion. Communication plays a crucial role in managing conflicts.

If money conflicts persist, one or both spouses may avoid discussing finances to prevent further disputes. However, this is not the best way to resolve conflicts. Avoiding discussions will only allow resentment to brew over time, eventually leading to an explosive confrontation. Healthy communication is the only solution to resolving money conflicts. If you find it challenging to manage these conflicts, consider seeking professional advice.

Challenges

If transparency is so vital in marriage, why do couples hesitate to share financial information? The reasons often stem from psychological, emotional, and social dynamics.

In Mahesh's case, he sought control over finances and wanted to avoid questions from his wife, thereby sidestepping potential conflicts. Aarav, on the other hand, concealed his loan out of guilt and shame for borrowing money for the wedding.

Some partners fear being judged for their financial habits or values. If one partner enjoys splurging while the other is more inclined to save, financial disagreements are common, making secrecy seem reasonable. They may hide financial issues to protect themselves emotionally, avoiding potential criticism or disappointment from their partner. Consequently, they may choose to talk less about money or avoid the topic altogether.

Harmony in Marriage

Communication and transparency are fundamental to achieving harmony in marriage. Without these elements, couples may accumulate wealth but still experience stress in their relationship. A stressful marriage can negatively impact the long-term well-being of the partnership. As discussed earlier, great wealth coupled with an unhappy marriage is not desirable. Harmony and financial stability in marriage must go hand in hand. Many marriages have faltered at this stage, but you, as a couple, can decide to prevent this from happening in your relationship.

> **"Communication and transparency are the second steps toward financial freedom and a happy marriage."**

Questions for Discussion:

1. What prevents each of you from sharing financial information? List your reasons honestly.

2. What steps will each of you take to become more

transparent?

3. Decide on a specific day and time each week, fortnight, or month to sit down and discuss your finances—budget, expenses, savings, and giving.

***

Bobby and Alka one year into their marriage had too many money conflicts. They decided to meet their marriage coach to find a solution for their conflicts.

"We have joint accounts. We are talking about money, I am transparent with her but she just doesn't understand me, I think" said Bobby.

"Neither does he! I think we are speaking different languages. Every word turns into arguments. I feel I am being judged for my expenses " said Alka.

"And I feel sometimes the word 'savings' is a bad word," said Bobby.

The coach took a deep breath, leaned back thoughtfully, and looked both into their eyes. "Interesting. Have you ever wondered why you have these silly arguments on spending and savings?"

"Why?" said both together.

"You need to know this third step, and many ignore this, just like you. If you know this step, it will be so liberating," said the advisor, who then immediately pointed to the board behind him, where the third step was written in bold.

STEP 3- KNOWING: "KNOW EACH OTHERS MONEY PERSONALITY"

Step Of Awareness – Self And Spouse

This section includes one chapter and covers money personalities and their impact on financial habits. Just as couples have distinct temperaments, they often differ in financial behaviours too, such as saving or spending. By understanding your and your spouse's money personality, you can foster a stronger partnership, enabling balanced decision-making, effective wealth-building, and a harmonious marriage journey.

Chapter 3
Same Money Different Mind

"Money personalities determine our financial habits, but unlike personality traits, they are not permanent and can be modified to become effective money managers."

I am choleric and melancholic, while my wife is sanguine and melancholic. You might be wondering now, what is that? I'll explain, but before that, let me get to the point. I knew my wife was an extrovert and I was an introvert, but beyond that, I didn't understand much about our personalities or temperaments. Four years into our marriage, we attended a family seminar where we learnt about the four temperaments, and that changed the way we thought about each other. This was the beginning of our journey toward self-awareness.

Essentially, there are four temperaments, and we usually exhibit a blend of two. Sanguines are extroverted, sociable, and exuberant. Melancholics are introverted, task-oriented, and perfectionistic. Cholerics are go-getters and type A personalities, also task-oriented. Phlegmatics are cool-headed, peace-loving, and unambitious. These temperaments are rooted in genetics and often remain unchanged.

Just as we have different temperaments and personalities, we also possess distinct money personalities, which this chapter will explore. This will be an important lesson in self-discovery and understanding your spouse, helping you navigate the challenges of managing money successfully.

Both Are Different

"You know we don't have sufficient savings for retirement, and a vacation is simply not on my priority list," Kyle said, raising his hands halfway while staring at Susan.

"What's the point of having a large retirement corpus if you won't have good memories and a loving partner during your much-anticipated retirement?" Susan replied, rolling her eyes and casting a sly smile in another direction.

Kyle preferred saving for the future and considered most spending unnecessary. Conversely, Susan believed that spending money to create memories with family took precedence over investing. So, who is right?

Both are right and wrong. Kyle was so focused on financial goals that he overlooked the relationships he needed to nurture. Susan was so intent on enjoying the present and creating memories that she neglected the importance of financial freedom at retirement. Why do they behave so differently? Because they have different money personalities.

Money Personality

In the story above, you likely guessed that Kyle is a saver and Susan is a spender. There are other personality types as well. Broadly speaking, we can categorise ourselves as savers, spenders, or givers. If we delve deeper, these personalities can branch out into many more. Psychologists believe there are numerous money personalities. I have compiled a list of the ten most common money personalities as follows:

The Saver: The saver prioritises long-term financial security, diligently setting aside funds for future goals and emergencies. They are generally frugal spenders who prefer to grow their savings and investments.

The Spender: The spender enjoys using money to enhance their lifestyle, frequently making purchases to satisfy immediate desires or emotional needs. They may struggle to adhere to a budget and often prioritise experiences over material goods.

The Giver: The giver derives satisfaction in using money to help others, whether through charitable contributions or providing for friends and family. They value making a positive impact over accumulating wealth for themselves.

The Status Seeker: The status seeker associates wealth with personal value and success. They often use money to purchase luxury items and project an image of wealth, sometimes at the expense of long-term financial stability.

The Money Monk: The Money Monk views money as an essential part of life but avoids becoming overly attached to it. They prioritise spiritual or personal fulfilment, live modestly, and place little value on material possessions.

The Risk Taker: The risk-taker enjoys high-stakes financial ventures and is willing to take significant risks for potentially large returns. This personality thrives on excitement and frequently engages in risky investments or participates in speculative markets.

The Investor: The investor is methodical and patient, focusing on long-term wealth accumulation through well-planned investments. They place a high value on financial education and are constantly seeking ways to maximise their investment returns.

The Avoider: The avoider avoids dealing with financial matters, often due to anxiety or fear of making mistakes. They may procrastinate on decisions about budgeting, saving, or debt management, hoping that problems will resolve themselves.

The Hoarder: The hoarder finds comfort in accumulating money, aggressively saving, and often hoarding resources out of fear of financial loss or instability. They may struggle to spend even on necessities.

The Hider: The Hider keeps their finances private, frequently concealing expenses or debts from their spouse or partner. This behaviour is motivated by a desire for control or a fear of being judged, but it can lead to trust issues in relationships.

Product of Influence

If you're wondering what leads to these differences in money personalities, several factors contribute to our financial behaviour. Unlike personality traits, which are a combination of genetics and upbringing, money personalities are shaped by different influences. One primary factor is what happens in which we grow up and how our parents display their attitudes toward money.

Children often imitate their parents, with whom they spend most of their formative years. The concept of money is imagined, visualised, and cultivated at home. If parents frequently discuss savings and demonstrate frugality, children are likely to adopt that lifestyle. Conversely, if parents talk about extravagant purchases and shop endlessly, children will likely absorb those habits. This is where money personalities are first formed.

After Dhruv married Anika, they decided to buy items for their home. Anika did most of the shopping while Dhruv was at work.

One day, after work, Dhruv noticed the price tags on some kitchen items and raised his eyebrows, saying, "Anika, don't you think this is expensive? I know a store that sells these items at lower prices. Can we buy from there?"

"I always look for quality, and what I've bought will last a long time," Anika replied with a grin, quickly pulling off the price tags from other items.

Dhruv's parents were very frugal due to his father's low salary. They saved diligently each month and spent carefully. In contrast, Anika's father worked for a government organisation and enjoyed a more abundant lifestyle at home. They were practicing what they had learnt in their respective households.

Besides family, societal influences, peer pressure, life circumstances, and financial literacy also shape one's personality.

For instance, if reading this book has a profound impact on you, your money personality may change as you begin implementing recommendations in this book.

Marriage of Two Opposites

The challenge in marriage arises when two partners possess different money personalities, which is often the case in many families. Imagine a saver marrying a spender. The saver husband constantly thinks about saving, while the spender wife is driven to spend. Their money values are opposites, leading to heightened tension when discussing or managing finances. Many homes have these typical challenges, but if not addressed properly, they can sour relationships. Each partner may believe they are superior, when the truth is none are. Each brings unique benefits and drawbacks to the table.

Couples rarely share the same money personality. As the saying goes, opposites attract, even when it comes to finances. Various combinations of different personalities exist in a marriage, each with its own unique characteristics, strengths, and weaknesses. As you read, you may recognise your own unique combination. Below is my list of different money personality combinations:

Couple	Super Savers	Balancers	Philanthropics	Spendthrifts	Two Extremes	Super Charitables
Husband	Saver	Spender	Giver	Spender	Giver	Giver
Wife	Saver	Saver	Saver	Spender	Spender	Giver

Couples money personality

Super Savers

A saver marries another saver. It's easy when it comes to saving. They typically share common financial goals. Because they save consistently, they often achieve financial freedom early in life. However, these families are not without challenges. Their primary issue may be rigid financial behaviour and an obsession with saving, which can prevent them from enjoying life despite having money, and would tend to compromise on charitable giving.

Balancers

A spender marries a saver, as seen in the story of Kyle and Susan. Such couples adopt a balanced approach to spending. When one partner tends to save excessively, the other leans toward spending, which can benefit the household. They complement each other, provided they are willing to appreciate one another. Challenges arise when they must prioritise their financial goals, leading to potential conflicts due to their opposing values.

Philanthropics

A giver marries a saver. These couples create wealth creators yet give substantial in charity. The saver ensures that money is invested wisely, allowing them to build wealth that can be donated at will. They naturally support each other, as their finances grow while also benefiting those in need. However, they may lack spontaneity and, like super savers, may have rigid financial behaviour.

Spendthrifts

A spender marries another spender. It's no surprise that this couple tends to spend more than they save or give. I consider this couple the most detrimental to the family's financial well-being, as spending takes precedence. However, not all is negative; spending can also be about creating memories rather than accumulating assets. Nevertheless, due to excessive spending, they are likely to find themselves in debt and face compromises at various life stages due to a lack of finances.

Two Extremes

A giver marries a spender. They are indeed extremes, but the flow of money is one-sided. One partner enjoys spending, while the other focuses on charitable giving. Both result in cash outflow, but one is self-serving while the other is selfless. This couple may enjoy both the joy of giving and the experiences spending brings, but they are likely to face cash crunches frequently, as money is consistently flowing out. Living on debt is a high possibility, and their priorities may be clearly diagonal.

Super Charitables

A giver marries another giver. Both partners love giving and philanthropy. However, their limitation is that since they do not save, their ability to donate is restricted to their current income. As their earning potential decreases later in life, their capacity to give diminishes. Although they are strong supporters of each other, they don't tend to enjoy life due to their selfless nature.

Self and Spouse Awareness

The key to resolving this tension lies in awareness—both self-awareness and spouse awareness. Each partner should know what is their own money personality and that of their spouse. Recognising the nuances, pros, and cons of each money personality helps couples appreciate their differences. It fosters an understanding that neither partner is superior; both bring unique strengths and weaknesses to the relationship.

In our first example, if Kyle had recognised his money personality, shaped by his upbringing, and understood that his wife had a different perspective due to her unique experiences, he would have responded differently. Additionally, he would have been more empathetic toward his wife's desire to spend on a vacation to create lasting memories, ultimately benefiting their relationship.

Knowledge of each other's money personality and open communication about feelings and expectations can foster a friendly dialogue. Over time, this understanding can lead to a stronger partnership, allowing each partner to grow. When one partner goes overboard, the other can help restore balance.

Complementary Couples

Akash enjoyed giving, while Shikha preferred saving. Akash was often moved to help those in need. One day, an old friend of Akash called him, sharing his dire situation. Without hesitation, Akash transferred Rs. 10,000 to him.

Later that day, he told Shikha, "My college friend called me and is going through a financial crisis. I gave him Rs. 10,000."

"But that extra cash was meant for investing! Why did you give it away without even consulting me?" Shikha replied, placing one hand on her forehead and frowning. She immediately left the room.

Akash was a giver, while Shikha was a saver. They represented a 'philanthropic' couple. Akash was compassionate and quick to give, while Shikha felt uncomfortable, fearing that Akash's generosity would jeopardise their savings and future investments.

One day, at a money seminar, they learnt about their money personalities and understood the reasons behind their differing behaviours. They exchanged glances when the speaker asked, "How many givers are here who are married to savers?" The speaker explained the challenges faced by such couples and how they could overcome them.

Later that month, Akash told Shikha about a need that arose at work. He first called her to ask if it was appropriate for him to give. Shikha also discussed her investment plans with Akash. Together, they created a plan for investing and giving, allowing each partner the freedom to pursue what they enjoyed most.

Money personalities are not permanent

Can money personalities change? Absolutely! There are numerous examples in life that demonstrate this. Our personalities are influenced by our genetic makeup and, to some extent, our upbringing. Money personalities, however, are primarily shaped by our environment and experiences, meaning they can be altered through external and internal changes.

My wife lost her father at a young age, just 14 years old. While her father was alive, they weren't so conscious of their expenses, as both her parents were working. After her father's death, they suddenly faced the struggle of living on half the income. She learnt to be frugal. When we married, she was careful with spending, while I was more of a spender. Over the years, she evolved into a saver. I, on the other hand, continued to spend until I met a financial planner. That day was an eyeopener, and I began saving aggressively.

For my wife, external circumstances changed her money personality, while for me, it was an internal transformation. My wife, along with her mother and sister, consciously started being cautious about spending, and I know for a fact that my mother-in-law was saving with an eye on her daughter's future. I also became aware of the substantial corpus I needed to build for our retirement and our children's education, which was the bare minimum. Today, we are both careful about spending, and saving and investing have become part of our lives.

While a spender cannot become a giver overnight, they can certainly learn to spend less, manage money better, and overtime learn to give. This transformation can occur when both partners support each other through the process. A family living in debt and extravagant spending can certainly change and begin managing money responsibly for a brighter future. It may be challenging for an individual to initiate this change, but a supportive and responsible spouse can work wonders.

Understanding each other's money personalities and cooperating with one another will undoubtedly foster harmony in the relationship and set you on the path to building wealth.

Understanding each other's money personalities is the third step toward growing your wealth and marriage together.

Questions for Discussion:
1. What is each of your money personalities, based on the ten listed in this chapter?

2. What are the top three challenges you face in managing money due to your different or similar money personality types?

3. Are there any decisions you would like to make to change aspects of your money personality that are creating conflict in your marriage?

***

T hey were old friends, meeting up at a cosy coffee shop. It was raining, and the sweet aroma of fresh coffee filled the air. They sat outside on the lawn under a large umbrella, enjoying the warmth of their drinks. As they settled in, the conversation began.

"So, how's the financial planning going? I heard you both have joint accounts now," Hari asked with a smile, leaning forward.

"Yes, we did that right after the seminar on money and marriage," Sam replied, his eyes lighting up. Jane added with a sly grin, "He even talks to me about money now!" They all laughed.

"What really opened my eyes was the session on personality," Hari said, his tone shifting to something more serious.

"You mean your money personality," Sarita teased with a smile, nudging him playfully.

"Right, right—money personality," Hari corrected himself, laughing at his slip-up.

Then his expression turned more earnest. "But the next step we took really saved us from going broke. We wouldn't have been able to afford even this cup of coffee if not for that."

Sam leaned in, eyes wide with curiosity and concern. "What happened?"

Sarita's voice trembled slightly with emotion as she spoke, glancing at her husband.

"I thank Hari for taking the initiative and getting that plan in place." Her eyes welled up with tears, a mix of gratitude and relief.

Hari looked at Sam and Jane, his expression sincere. "Remember the plan we talked about—the fourth step?"

STEP 4- PROTECTING: "PLAN YOUR RISK"

Step Of Mitigating

This section contains two chapters. The first emphasises the importance of risk planning and insurance in financial preparedness for emergencies. Planning involves mitigating financial risks through insurance to protect loved ones, as illustrated by stories of families facing hardship. The second, highlights the importance of health insurances as a shield for your wealth, essential for protecting saings from rising hospital costs. Emergency funds provide additional support, reducing stress. Risk planning ensures financial stability, fostering peace within families.

Chapter 4

Ignoring a Risk Plan is Risky

"Emergencies in life are uncertain, but planning for emergencies should be certain."

In just over four months, she spent Rs. 1.80 crore to keep her husband alive. He was battling for breath, fighting COVID pneumonia in a hospital in India. After reading an article on Indiatimes.com it became clear that she spent most of their savings to save the life of the man she dearly loved. Thank God he survived, but that came at a tremendous cost. There are countless stories of hospitalisation during COVID. Many families have spent five, ten, twenty, or even thirty lakhs. Some hospitals charged as much as Rs. one lakh per day for hospitalization. This situation underscores the importance of financial preparedness. While we cannot control health crises, we can certainly control how well we are financially equipped to handle them.

According to an article published in India Today, 40 crore Indians are just one medical emergency away from financial ruin. This statistic highlights the lack of awareness or importance that many people in India place on insurance. This issue is not limited to rural India. In a survey I conducted among 76 families in urban India in the age bracket 25 to 50 years, 80% of respondents lacked any form of insurance.

Probability and Consequences

The pandemic taught many lessons to this generation, with the most significant being the importance of managing risk. Large-scale hospitalisations left many families without a breadwinner, forcing them to navigate financial challenges without adequate support. Before the world.

Until then, everyone thought uncertainty in life was manageable because the probability of adverse events was low. However, during COVID, that probability surged dramatically. The pandemic taught us that while the likelihood of an event occurring may be low, the consequences can be severe.

For example, during the pandemic, hospital bills skyrocketed. Most families were accustomed to bills ranging from fifty thousand to a couple of lakhs in the pre-COVID era, but during the pandemic, those costs increased tenfold. No one was prepared for such exorbitant expenses.

In 2021, within a month, I received WhatsApp forwards about at least ten young men I knew who died from COVID-19. No one expected men in their twenties and thirties to die. So no one was particularly devastating for young wives with small children. Most of these families lacked life insurance, which could have provided financial protection for their loved ones. The magnitude of the consequences was too high.

Avoidable Bitter Experiences

Was this situation avoidable? Absolutely! While the spread of the pandemic was unavoidable, the financial calamities that followed were largely preventable. A simple plan could have made a significant difference, and that is the objective of this chapter: to emphasise the importance of a 'risk plan." Many don't think of risk planning until they are compelled by life circumstances. Let us explore the significance of risk planning in financial management and how it can safeguard your family's future in emergencies.

Importance of Risk Planning

In 2001, following the Sept. 11 terrorist attacks, Warren Buffet wrote in the Berkshire Hathaway annual report. Warren Buffet writes this:

"Why, you might ask, didn't I recognise the above facts before September 11th? The answer, sadly, is that I did—but I didn't convert thought into action. I violated the Noah rule: Predicting rain doesn't count; building arks does."

The story of Noah from the Bible illustrates this principle. God pours down rain for 40 days and nights due to the wickedness among his people, but Noah and his family were safe in the ark he built on God's instructions because he was a righteous man. Warren Buffet, a long-term investor, referenced this quote in the context of risk planning in investing, which is equally applicable to personal finances. He meant that it is not enough to foresee potential risks; one must also take steps to mitigate these challenges.

"Risk planning involves preparing for unexpected events that could jeopardise your financial security, assessing their likelihood, and creating plans to minimise their impact. It ensures that individuals are prepared for unforeseen events like illness, accidents, or job loss, helping to protect their finances and future. Let us delve into the details of each component of risk planning and how it can protect your wealth.

Meaning of Insurance

When we were seven months into our marriage, I received a decent bonus. We used part of that bonus to buy our first scooter—an automatic Honda Activa for Rs. 40,000. As newlyweds, we were not accustomed to riding scooters, so I purchased helmets for both of us. You might wonder why I bought two helmets. It was a form of family insurance. We knew we wouldn't fall often, but if we did, our heads would be protected. This was our first step in risk planning together.

Let me begin with insurance, which is the cornerstone of every risk plan.

Life is uncertain even in normal times. Illness and death can strike anyone at any time, although the probability is low for young families. This uncertainty becomes even more acute during crises.

For instance, during a war, civil unrest, or a looming health crisis like a pandemic, uncertainties can take a toll on our emotions, mental health, and finances. While emotional and health challenges can be managed over time, financial difficulties can become overwhelming, especially for families with low incomes or those who have not yet built wealth. This is where insurance plays a crucial role in the lives of an individual or family.

Insurance essentially involves transferring risk to an insurance company in exchange for a premium. This risk can relate to injury, health issues, or life. Therefore, if there is a financial loss due to hospitalisation or death, the insurance company compensates the policyholder.

Term Insurance: Protecting Your Family's Future

Ketan was 38 years old when he died from complications, leaving behind Sania, 36, a homemaker, and their 3-year-old son, Samit. Sania was devastated and found it hard to believe. She missed Ketan deeply and was overwhelmed by thoughts of the future. The prospect of providing for Samit weighed heavily on her mind. Ketan had made some investments in property and fixed deposits, but hospitalisation expenses depleted their savings, leaving her with limited resources and the urgent need to find a job.

Death is inevitable, and most people pass away in old age when their children are grown and they have reasonably good savings so that even if the breadwinner dies, the family can survive and meet financial goals. While the probability of dying young is less, the consequences can be severe, as illustrated by Ketan's case.

During the pandemic, many young men died, leaving behind young wives and little children. While the emotional loss is irreplaceable, the financial loss could have been avoided. I heard numerous stories of families lacking sufficient savings and relying on support from relatives and friends.

To mitigate such risks, term insurance is essential. Ketan, in our example, never thought of term insurance. He could have easily afforded a cover of one crore for just Rs. 12,000 per annum when he got married at 29. It's not that he didn't love his wife; he simply lacked the foresight to secure their future.

A term insurance policy is a pure insurance product. The premium is low, but the coverage is substantial. A simple way to determine how much term insurance you need is to multiply the primary earner's yearly salary by 15 or 20. This amount ensures that the family remains financially stable if the worst occurs.

Take a moment to reflect on your family's situation. Do you have a financial safety net in place to protect them if the unthinkable happens? If not, now is the time to take action. If you are a husband reading this, I strongly recommend that you consider purchasing term insurance urgently. Discuss this matter with your wife and consult a financial advisor or insurance agent to determine how much coverage you need. This can be an emotional discussion, and not everyone enjoys having these conversations. However, it is better to address this now and take prompt action, as the consequences of inaction can lead to far greater emotional hardship.

Purpose of Term Insurance

A term insurance policy essentially replaces the breadwinner's current salary and accounts for what they would have saved if they were alive. The proceeds from the policy should ensure that the spouse can invest and earn returns for the rest of their life. In addition, it should cover any outstanding loans, children's higher education, and wedding expenses.

No one can compensate for the emotional trauma a family experiences after a loss, and insurance is never meant to do that. However, it can prevent the family from facing further stress and trauma due to financial struggles. The financial burden following a tragedy can amplify emotional distress, making it harder for families to heal. Risk planning can provide a sense of security, allowing families to focus on recovery rather than worrying about bills.

Sumer died of a heart attack at just 42 years old, leaving behind his 40-year-old wife, Sarita, and their 12-year-old daughter, Alia. While mourning her husband's death, a close friend of Sumer, who was also their financial advisor, visited their home and shared something that changed the course of their lives.

"We are sorry for your loss. It's hard to believe Sumer is no longer with us."

The advisor continued, "I just wanted to inform you, if you didn't know, that Sumer purchased a term insurance policy for two crores."

"The insurance company will settle this claim soon; they just need his death certificate. Whenever it's possible, please share a copy, and I will handle the paper work."

Upon hearing these simple yet profound statements, Sarita's eyes filled with tears, and she began to weep. She was moved by her husband's thoughtfulness and love. She felt relieved and confident that she wouldn't have to worry about her daughter's future—her education and marriage. She silently whispered, "Sumer, I love you, and thank you for caring for us even from afar."

Term insurance provides a payout after you *leave* this world, but the insurance you are about to read is designed for your lifetime while you *live* in this world, and it deserves the attention it warrants.

Chapter 5

Health Insurance is Wealth Insurance

"Health is wealth. When you insure against hospitalisation, you are essentially protecting your wealth"

During my time at Alliance Capital Mutual Fund (now Alliance Bernstein), a U.S. based asset management company, I underwent a minor surgery for a deviated nasal septum (DNS) in 2001. Upon returning to the office after my surgery, my boss informed me, "Submit all your bills; your hospitalisation is covered." I was initially confused but pleasantly surprised. I later received reimbursement for all my hospital expenses. I found myself wondering why the company would go to such lengths for me.

This experience marked my introduction to the world of health insurance. While I didn't need the money, I felt immense relief. How much more significant is this for those who cannot afford hospitalisation expenses?

Health Insurance: Shielding Your Savings

Like term insurance, health insurance is a pure insurance product that transfers the risk of health-related expenses and hospitalisation to the insurance company. Hospitalisation costs have skyrocketed in recent times, and we will all eventually require it. Without insurance, these substantial expenses must be drawn from savings and long-term investments, disrupting your financial goals and hindering your wealth-building journey. Thus, a health insurance policy serves to protect your wealth.

During the COVID-19 health crisis, many individuals lost their entire savings to hospital bills, while others had to borrow or rely on the generosity of donors. I recall numerous WhatsApp forwards detailing those in dire need of financial assistance due to hospitalization. Covid-19 was a unique situation, and many stepped forward to help, which may not occur during normal circumstances.

An adequate health policy is, therefore, a prudent approach to managing personal and family finances. As the average age of a family increases, the need for higher coverage becomes essential. Every family should consider a family floater policy, with coverage in the range of Rs. five to ten lakhs being a must.

Company-Sponsored Policies

Most employees have access to company-sponsored health insurance, but this policy typically expires once they leave the company. The employee may then receive a new policy from their new employer. While this may seem straightforward, it presents a problem. What if the employee is terminated and takes time to secure another job? What if they require hospitalisation during this gap? Although the probability may be low, the potential consequences are significant. Hospital bills would then need to be paid out of pocket, which can severely impact savings.

Upon retirement, most company-sponsored policies do not transfer to individuals working for private firms. Retired employees must then purchase a new health insurance policy, often carrying the burden of lifestyle diseases acquired during their working years. Conditions such as diabetes, hypertension, and heart-related issues are common. Acquiring a policy in retirement can be prohibitively expensive. Moreover, as you age, the need for health insurance only increases.

In fact, even when you are young, an insurance company may refuse to provide a health insurance policy due to pre-existing conditions. I personally know individuals in their forties who have been denied health insurance or faced exorbitantly high premiums.

Self-Sponsored Insurance

To mitigate these risks, every couple should purchase their own health insurance policy for the family. It is advisable to buy health insurance while you are still healthy and young, even if it means opting for lower coverage initially. Coverage can be increased annually at renewal. Later in life, even after many years, any new health issues will still be covered under the same policy without additional premiums.

Every family should assess their unique needs based on age and financial capacity to determine the appropriate policy. A financial advisor can assist in identifying the right coverage for your family. The higher the average age of the family, the greater the coverage should be.

Safe keeping and records

While selecting the right insurance is crucial, it is equally important to ensure that all original policies and documents are securely stored. In many families, the husband typically takes the lead in purchasing insurance, but little attention is given to discussing the types of insurance held and the location of the original documents. Both aspects are essential—safeguarding the documents and ensuring that both partners know where they are stored. These documents should be kept securely at home or in a bank locker, depending on what is most convenient. As your children grow older, it is your responsibility to discuss these matters with them and inform them about the insurance policies you have purchased and where they are safely stored.

In March 2021, I took my first flight after more than a year of lockdown and restrictions. For the first time in my life, I felt that the chances of my passing away sooner rather than later were higher. Before boarding the flight, I arranged a discussion with my wife and my two daughters to share details about all our insurance policies, emergency funds, bank accounts, and investments. I felt a sense of relief before taking that flight. Thankfully, I survived the pandemic, but what I shared with my family remains invaluable

Emergency Funds—your safety net

In January 2020, just before the pandemic struck, my father passed away unexpectedly. I had to fly to Udupi, in southern Karnataka, for the funeral. Within a couple of hours, we decided to travel as a family. It was indeed a family emergency, and I booked flight tickets for my wife and two daughters to accompany me. Fortunately, I had liquid cash available in mutual funds. I used my card to book the tickets and later repaid the amount using those liquid funds – my emergency fund.

In addition to transferring risk to insurance companies, there is one final aspect of emergency preparedness known as the emergency fund. An emergency fund is also a form of risk management, but something that the family has to build using your own financial resources.

The purpose of an emergency fund is to provide financial support during uncertainties or emergencies, so you don't have to dip into your long-term investments or take out loans. Having an emergency fund alleviates the stress on your family to arrange funds at short notice.

The size of an emergency fund is typically three to six months' worth of your essential monthly expenses, allowing you to meet those needs during times of crisis. Common emergencies include job loss, major unexpected home repairs, illnesses not covered by health insurance, and emergency travel. An emergency fund isn't just for significant life events like job loss; it can also cover urgent medical bills that insurance doesn't cover or even unexpected expenses like car repairs when you need it most.

Job loss is one of the biggest of them all. I would say depending on how quickly you can secure a new job, this should determine the size of your emergency fund. For instance, if you believe you can find a new job easily, a fund covering three to six months of expenses may suffice. However, if you think it will take longer to find a new job, you may want to have a more substantial emergency fund—covering six months to a year.

Lack of preparedness

An article in the Times of India, a leading newspaper in India, mentions that "75% of Indians don't have an emergency fund." This survey was conducted by Finology Ventures, a personal finance platform in India. The report titled 'India's Money Habits' also states that "82% of life insurance holders don't have adequate coverage, and 20% of health insurance holders lack sufficient coverage."

The survey I referenced earlier, out of 76 young families, 58 families (76%) did not have an emergency fund. It is evident that many families in India do not take risk planning seriously until a tragedy takes place when it is too late. This realisation typically comes only after the incident has transpired. This sense of urgency should be a constant presence in your family, driving you to secure term insurance, health insurance, and build your emergency fund.

Stress in the Family

The stress a family experiences and its impact on relationships is often underestimated. A young family already faces adjustments early in marriage, and financial stress of finances is only an additional burden that significantly affects relationships. Lack of preparedness for emergencies can lead to unnecessary actions and decisions, the most common being taking out loans. We will discuss loans in detail in a subsequent chapter.

By taking a few simple steps today—such as securing term insurance, health insurance, and establishing an emergency fund—you can safeguard your family's future and enjoy peace of mind, knowing you are prepared for life's uncertainties. A happy family is one where conflicts are minimised, and definitely having good risk planning is essential.

> *Planning your risks is the fourth step in growing your wealth and nurturing your marriage together.*

Questions for Discussion:

1. Do you believe your family has adequate insurance and emergency funds?

2. Do you plan to make any changes to your risk plan?

3. What other types of insurance do you think your family might need besides term and health insurance?

***

Sudhir and Asha had been married for twenty years and had two sons. Last month, Sudhir had gone through a major hospitalisation, and while he was now recovering, it had been a challenging time for the family. Rajesh, their long-time friend and financial advisor, visited them to check on Sudhir's recovery and to go over their finances.

Rajesh sat on the sofa, opened his laptop, and pulled up their portfolio.

"I'm glad to see your mutual fund portfolio is doing well, and that your recent hospitalisation didn't affect it," Rajesh said with a smile.

Then, with a more serious tone, he added, "So, how important do you think your decision about risk planning was?"

"Crucial," Sudhir nodded. "When you advised me to buy health insurance and build an emergency fund, I thought it was unnecessary. I even told Asha I didn't want to go ahead with it."

Sudhir continued, "But she insisted we follow your plan. At the time, I felt like I was just ticking another box. But last month, when I saw those hospital bills, I realised just how important that decision was."

"You are right!" Sudhir said, a look of relief on his face. "My hospitalisation didn't affect our portfolio at all."

Rajesh leaned forward. "I also wanted to remind you about your financial goals—specifically the one approaching next year."

"Yes, Rohan's college fees," Sudhir said.

"I still remember that first meeting when you asked us what we thought college fees would be like. You showed us how much they'd rise in 16 years with inflation, and we laughed, thinking it couldn't possibly get that high."

"I checked the other day, Rajesh—you were right," Sudhir admitted.

Asha chimed in, "Thanks to the fifth step, we have confidence we'll have enough for retirement and all our other goals. We've been following everything you taught us."

Rajesh smiled, clearly proud. "I appreciate your sincerity and that you remember the fifth step. Trust me, it's been the game-changer for everyone who has taken it seriously."

STEP 5– PLANNING: "HAVE COMMON FINANCIAL GOALS"

Step to Financial Freedom

This section covers three chapters. Chapter one covers inspiring stories of health and financial transformations driven by disciplined planning, goal-setting, and resilience. Setting specific, shared financial goals fosters stability and peace. Chapter two covers how wealth is built over time by investing rather than just saving. Financial terms like compounding and inflation are discussed with real life examples. Family goals, like home ownership, education, weddings, and retirement planning are explained. Chapter three is focused on target savings for various financial goals. For long-term goals like retirement or education, investing systematically, considering inflation, and maintaining asset allocation are crucial for financial stability and growth.

Chapter 6
Our Plans Our Goals

"Financial goals provide direction for a family to manage, and grow their wealth. Without goals, couples may find themselves aimless, often in debt, and inclined towards spending"

This story of transformation from the Times of India in October 2023 caught my attention. Ashish Sachdeva underwent a remarkable weight loss transformation, shedding 61 kg over 2.5 years after starting at 140 kg at age 36. He made lifestyle changes and followed a specific diet *plan* that included strength training, cardio workouts, and yoga in his routine. When asked how he maintained focus, he stated, "I have a strong belief system. I set SMART (Specific, Measurable, Achievable, Relevant, and Time-bound) goals for myself."

Numerous such transformation stories exist. One source is the National Weight Control Registry, which features individuals like Don Kaufman, who started as an obese son of an obese mother and lost 70 pounds by age 78. Dacia Gill lost

110 pounds, and Pat Holmes lost 114 pounds. Raul Robles lost 140 pounds. All were once overweight and have since lost significant amounts of pounds. The common thread in these stories is a diet and exercise plan. They all had a goal—they were determined to lose weight and regain their health. Every one of them had challenges or life-threatening diseases but ultimately reversed their health issues and emerged victorious.

What enabled them to achieve their weight when all odds were against them? Goals and a plan. Can such transformation stories occur in personal finance? Can a family with poor financial health, significant debt, and no savings transform into a wealthy family? Absolutely! There is no doubt, and there are a number of transformation stories that exist in personal finance. If you are seeking a change in your financial situation, keep reading this chapter. There are many ideas and approaches that can forever alter your destiny. For all transformations—whether in health, relationships, or finances—you need long-term discipline, planning, and perseverance.

Goals and Planning

Jim Rohn, the famous entrepreneur, author, and motivational speaker, said this:

> "If you go to work on your goals, your goals will go to work on you. If you go to work on your plan, your plan will go to work on you. Whatever good things we build end up building us."

Most people underestimate the impact of goals and plans in life. If you want to achieve anything worthwhile, you need goals. Your goals shape your future and help you attain what you desire. What happens to those who lack goals? They receive not what they want, but what they deserve. Health goals, professional goals, family goals, spiritual goals, and many others should be integral to everyone's life. There is no doubt that if you want to grow your wealth and avoid debt, you need a solid financial plan in place. This plan should be a shared financial plan.

Inevitable and planned

Whenever I pose the question in seminars on financial planning, "What are your financial goals?" Most attendees mention buying a house, a car, funding children's higher education, and other aspirations. Very few mention retirement. If there is one goal that is inevitable, it is retirement, yet practically everyone I have met does not have a plan for it. There are other significant goals for our children that we all aspire to, although not everyone actively plans for them. These include funding children's higher education and children's wedding. Whether you save or not, you will inevitably spend money on these events.

Additionally, there are aspirations that you may feel compelled to pursue due to external pressures. For instance, you may want to buy a house or a car because you feel pressured to keep up with your colleagues or relatives. Some individuals have a mission in life that becomes a goal, such as establishing schools or hospitals in underserved areas after retirement. These aspirations require substantial funds, necessitating advance planning, sometimes many years ahead.

In Control

Effective long-term planning empowers couples to maintain control over their financial decisions rather than being forced into undesirable choices that could have negative consequences later. All these goals have financial implications. There are only two ways to fund these events or choices: either use your own saved money or borrow. It's that simple. If you plan, you save and can purchase using your own funds. If you don't plan, borrowing becomes the only option. Later in the chapter on debt, we will discuss the detrimental effects of loans on both marriage and wealth creation. Thus, a plan helps you take control.

Goals and Harmony

Ryan and Jennifer, early in their marriage, decided they would manage their finances separately while contributing to common household expenses. One day, Jennifer called her financial advisor to discuss her plans to invest in mutual funds.

"Can you both let me know your preferred day and time for discussions?" asked Sarah, the financial advisor.

"No, that's fine. He manages his own investments, and I manage mine. The house we purchased is on a joint home loan. I know he has invested in mutual funds, so I thought I would explore these new investment options," Jennifer replied.

As mentioned earlier, these goals are not individual but common goals. A husband and wife should collaboratively plan these goals, even though the process may not always be smooth. Conflicts and disagreements are likely to arise, but they must work toward common objectives. This is an opportunity for both partners to listen to each other, share ideas, and express their thoughts, whether they agree or disagree. This also allows the less active partner to engage in discussions about financial matters.

When Kishan's financial advisor suggested including his wife Anika in their financial planning call, he initially thought her presence was unnecessary. However, the advisor insisted. During the call, Anika asked more questions than Kishan, surprising him. At the end of the call, she expressed her gratitude to the advisor.

"Thank you for including me in the call. I trust Kishan, but knowing all this about investments and money management was fascinating. I will support my husband in our wealth-building plan," Anika told the advisor.

Financial goals must be agreed upon by both partners, as seen in the case of Kishan and Anika. If a husband and wife cannot reach a consensus on their financial goals, consulting a financial coach can provide guidance and support.

Financial freedom and a strong marriage stem from effective planning and partnership—a shared desire to grow and move in the same direction. While couples can pursue separate financial goals and achieve individual success, this approach may be successful individually, but that will never build or strengthen their marriage. Ultimately, it may serve personal interests rather than the partnership, leading to a poor future.

Different Plans

There are three major categories for a common financial plan that couples can outline:

1. Spending Plan

2. Risk Plan

3. Investment Plan

Risk planning warranted a separate chapter, so we will focus on *spending* in this chapter and *investment planning* in the next, as they are closely linked.

Budgeting and Spending

Charles A. Jaffe, a personal finance columnist at the Boston Globe, states,

> "It's not your salary that makes you rich; it's your spending habits."

This statement rings true. Spending habits are crucial for building wealth. Controlling and monitoring spending is essential for achieving this goal. There is no better method than preparing a budget and tracking expenses.

Expenses fall into two categories: living expenses and lifestyle expenses. Living expenses are necessary for survival; without them, life can become challenging. These include groceries, rent, and transportation. Lifestyle expenses, on the other hand, are not essential for living but contribute to maintaining a certain lifestyle, such as clothing purchases or vacations.

Budgeting Process

Even before marriage, I developed the habit of budgeting, likely due to financial constraints. My first salary was Rs. 1200 back in 1992, and I had to manage my expenses carefully. Thankfully, during that time, easy loans, EMIs, and credit cards were not prevalent. The only way to manage money was through budgeting.

After getting married, I continued this practice with my wife. Just before our wedding, I took out a home loan, which forced us to live on a tight budget. Shortly after the wedding, I had no savings left. A friend of ours, who did the woodwork and renovation for our new house, kindly allowed us to defer payment. This situation compelled us to save money each month, as there was no other option but to stick to the budget.

If you have never prepared a budget, start today. This habit will ultimately help you build wealth. If you're unsure how to begin, don't worry; it's straightforward, and anyone can do it. It requires discipline and a willingness to cultivate a good habit.

Pull your credit card and UPI transactions from the past three months and compile them on an Excel sheet. This is a good starting point. Additionally, make a list of all your cash expenses that you can recall, assigning labels to each expense (e.g., groceries, petrol, electricity bill, etc.). You will have fixed and variable expenses. Fixed expenses are easy to remember and do not require control, such as rent, school fees, and insurance premiums. Variable expenses, however, require monitoring to ensure you don't exceed your budget, such as groceries or dining out.

John Maxwell says,

> "A budget is telling your money where to go instead of wondering where it went."

Dave Ramsey, America's leading financial coach, adds,

> "Budgeting is the process of creating a spending plan for your money. By creating this spending plan, you can determine in advance whether you will have enough money to do the things you need or want to do."

A well-structured budget will guide your spending and purchases, preventing unnecessary purchases and helping you track expenses effectively. Budgeting is a fundamental exercise in financial planning. Without a budget, saving, investing, or building wealth becomes nearly impossible.

Mastering spending your greatest asset

Mastering your spending through budgeting will become your greatest asset in wealth building. Without planning your financial goals, you cannot effectively plan your spending. Planning helps determine the resources required for each goal and how to manage reaching these goals with limited resources. When resources are limited, spending automatically reduces. With lack of budgeting, overspending becomes common, leading to reduced savings.

If wealth is your destination, your journey begins with the first step—budgeting. It creates the opportunity to save and build a solid foundation. However, the real adventure begins with the next step—investment planning. Both are essential; you cannot reach your goals without taking both steps. Now that your 'Budgeting Flight' has safely landed, it's time to board the 'Investment Planning Flight.' I assure you, this part of the journey will be more thrilling—and far more rewarding.

Chapter 7
Investing is slow and Fast

"How many millionaires do you know who have become wealthy by investing in savings accounts? I rest my case." — Robert G. Allen

In his book 'The Psychology of Money,' Morgan Housel introduces a man named Ronald Read and narrates his fascinating story. He writes:

Read worked at a gas station for 25 years and swept floors at JCPenney for 17 years. He bought a two-bedroom house for $12,000 at age 38 and lived there for the rest of his life. Widowed at age 50, he never remarried. A friend recalled that his main hobby was chopping firewood. Read died in 2014 at age 92. Which is when the humble rural janitor made international headlines.

In his will, the former janitor left $2 million to his stepchildren and more than $6 million to his local hospital and library.

Those who knew Read were baffled. Where did he amass such wealth? It turned out there was no secret. He didn't win the lottery or inherit money. Read saved what little he could and invested it in blue-chip stocks, patiently waiting for decades as his modest savings compounded into over $8 million. That's the story—from janitor to philanthropist.

This chapter focuses on multiplying and building your wealth. There are two fundamental steps to wealth creation: reduce spending and increase investments. While budgeting helps control spending, investment planning enhances returns. Simply saving more does not automatically lead to wealth growth. In fact, savings alone do not create wealth; they merely provide an opportunity to build it. Wealth is built through investing gradually, as exemplified by Ronald Read. Before delving into the details of investment planning, let's clarify some essential financial terms that everyone should understand.

Savings and investing

Savings and investing are distinct concepts. Savings lay the groundwork for investing. Savings are typically for the short term, yielding low returns with minimal risk, and are highly liquid—allowing for immediate withdrawal. Keeping money in a home safe or a savings account is an example of savings. Conversely, investments are intended for the long term, offering higher returns at greater risk, often with lower liquidity or penalties for early withdrawal. Investing in mutual funds or real estate exemplifies long-term investment. Investing requires patience, as it often appears slow, but it can yield significant returns, making it both slow and fast.

Inflation and the Time Value of Money

During one of my trips to Mumbai, I stayed with a dear friend whose father was a captivating storyteller. He recounted his first job in Mumbai in the 1960s as a teenager. He left his hometown in southern India and travelled to Mumbai for work. He proudly stated, "I earned Rs. 2 daily and received 25 paise in tips. I could buy a rice plate for 50 paise and bhajia pav and chai for 4 annas (each anna is 6 paise)." Fast forward to 2024, and there is no longer a 25 paise coin, while the Rs. 2 coin is exchanged without a second thought. This illustrates the impact of inflation on money.

As a school kid in the 70s, I vividly remember buying a 5-Star Cadbury chocolate for Rs. 5 (five rupees). If my memory serves me right, it was the 45 gm size. I don't recall any other brand. Later, Dairy milk chocolate was added to the mix. Today, that same chocolate likely costs Rs. 35. This is inflation at work. Inflation refers to the rising costs year after year, causing money to lose its value. Ten years ago, what you could purchase for Rs. 1000 would now cost you Rs. 2000 at an inflation rate of approximately 7%. As of writing, India's inflation rate hovers between 5% and 6% (2024).

Consequently, if your returns fall below 6%, you are effectively losing money each year. So, the goal is to earn returns exceeding 6% to grow your wealth incrementally. Thus, achieving investment returns becomes crucial for wealth building. Beating inflation is essential for maintaining healthy financials. While everyone desires higher returns, achieving them often requires taking on greater risk.

Compounding

Compounding is another critical element in long-term investments. You may be familiar with the concept of compound interest. While simple interest is calculated solely on the principal amount year on year. Compound interest is calculated on both the principal and accumulated interest, leading to exponential growth over time. Imagine a snowball rolling downhill; the further it travels, the larger it becomes. Compounding operates similarly. This principle is vital for long-term investments, as returns can become exponential after several years, thanks to the accumulation of interest on interest. For example, if you invested Rs. one lakh 20 years ago at a 10% interest rate, its current value would be Rs. 6.70 lakhs. In contrast, simple interest would yield only Rs. 2 lakhs. The combination of time and interest rates is what transformed one lakh into over six lakhs.

Financial goals

Now that we have explored some of the basic financial terms, let's delve into the concept of financial goals. Every family must plan their financial goals, as they are inevitable events in life, whether planned or not. Planning streamlines these goals and optimises the resources required to achieve them. Common financial goals for families have are buying a house, a car, funding children's higher education, planning for weddings, and philanthropic endeavours.

In my early forties, my company arranged for a meeting with a financial planner, which proved to be a turning point in our lives. The trajectory of our finances changed hugely. I shared my income and expense statement with the planner, and what he revealed on his laptop remains vivid in my memory. He listed all the important financial goals and used an Excel sheet and computed the necessary funds. When he shared the final sheet, I was momentarily taken aback. For the first time in our married life, I realised we were struggling financially. History often repeats itself; now, as a certified financial planning professional (CFP®), I observe similar reactions from my clients.

Why did I feel we were doing poorly financially, or why do my clients feel the same? It's because only after working out the financial goals do we realise how much we need for each goal and how much we must save to achieve them. My current savings were insufficient, and my salary at the time did not allow for adequate savings for all our financial goals. I will explain more details below. But first, let's take a quick look at typical financial goals and how they influence every family's journey toward building wealth.

Buying a House

Every young family aspires to own a home. Early in marriage, few families possess all the financial resources needed to purchase a house, leading them to seek home loans. We bought our home even before getting married and took out a home loan. Home loans are rarely granted for the full value of the property; a down payment of 10-20% is typically required from the borrower. Thus, the down payment becomes a *financial goal*. Loan tenures can range from two to thirty years, with anything less than five years being termed short-term.

As a financial planner, I strongly advise young families to consider purchasing their first home only after ten years of marriage. Families should first focus on building wealth through long-term investment products like equities. By following this strategy, you may end up buying a house with your own funds or with a much smaller loan while simultaneously building long-term wealth.

Buying a two or four-wheeler

In today's generation, purchasing two-wheelers or four-wheelers has become so common that many families purchase them early in their marriage, often without sufficient funds. Consequently, they frequently resort to loans. I strongly recommend against purchasing a two or four-wheeler with a loan. In the next chapter, I have covered in detail what the long-term impact of such decisions is on wealth creation. Instead, consider making the purchase of a two- or four-wheeler a financial goal.

Children's Education

Most parents I have spoken with keep the financial goal of funding their children's education in the back of their minds but never technically plan for it. This is understandable, as the need seems distant. Many parents believe they will have enough money saved by the time their children reach college.

This line of thinking is flawed because the need only compounds over time due to inflation. While general inflation in India is currently between 5% and 6%, education inflation is around 10%. Therefore, establishing a financial goal for children's education should be a top priority for any family. The only alternative is to rely on education loans.

My wife and I also assumed we would have enough funds when our children grew older, but the financial planner revealed the reality. That day, I doubted whether we would have sufficient funds for our children's education. Thankfully, we took immediate action and made the right investments, and today we are confident that we have enough funds for their higher studies.

Children's Weddings

I am personally not a proponent of extravagant and ostentatious weddings. In India, weddings are significant events, and families often spend beyond their means. Borrowing for weddings is common, yet this is one of the most regrettable types of loans. I have shared more about this in the next chapter.

I strongly advise families to avoid overspending on weddings and to establish a financial goal for this purpose. Without such a goal, you may end up depleting your retirement corpus or taking on substantial loans for wedding expenses. I have encountered families who have thoughtlessly overspent on weddings and now lack sufficient funds for retirement.

Philanthropy

Many individuals express a desire to establish schools, hospitals, or other initiatives that serve society. I'm sure you also harbour such aspirations. Giving back to society is a noble goal that many keep hidden in their hearts. The only way to fulfil this dream is to set it as a financial goal. It is impossible to achieve this dream without documenting it as a financial objective.

Retirement

Last but not least! I consider retirement one of the most critical financial goals. Improved medical care, better diets, and healthier lifestyles have increased life expectancy. Life expectancy refers to the average number of years a person can expect to live.

According to an article on macrotrends.net, life expectancy in India was 45 years in 1960, meaning people could expect to live a maximum of 45 years. By 2020, it reached 70 years, and post-pandemic, it stands at 68 years as of 2022. This increase indicates that after the official retirement age of 60, individuals can expect to live an additional 20–25 years, requiring a regular income during a period when they are no longer employed.

Retirement years are particularly vulnerable. You are not at your peak physically or mentally, and your skills may be outdated, making it challenging to find employment that provides a regular income. Logically, it is unwise to rely on loans for emergencies. Children are focused on their own career advancements and wealth accumulation during this stage of their lives.

It's only fair to invest for retirement, considering you have your entire lifetime to save and invest. Establishing a financial goal from the moment you start earning is essential. As a young couple, you need to save a relatively small amount for this goal, and because of compounding over the years, you will accumulate a substantial corpus.

But what if the corpus you anticipated turns out to be insufficient during your retirement years? Remember, you can't apply for a job at that stage. Therefore, it is crucial to keep your eyes on the target.

Chapter 8

All eyes on the bull's eye

"People save blindly and randomly without knowledge of their financial goals and the exact amount of money required."

In 2012, my family and I went on vacation to the USA. There were four of us, and fortunately, my mother-in-law lives there, so we didn't have to pay for the stay. However, we still needed to plan for our visa, flight tickets from Hyderabad to Florida and back, as well as visits to friends and relatives in Pennsylvania and New York City.

We began planning a year in advance, in 2011. While I don't recall the exact amount spent, our plan included USA visa fees, flight tickets, cab fares, and other incidental expenses during our stay. This became our financial goal, with the expenses serving as the target amount.

Financial Goal: Target Savings

There were two ways to fund this trip: either save every month until the travel date or withdraw from our short-term savings. I had some savings in the bank, and the rest I saved from my monthly salary. Let's assume we spent Rs. three lakhs in total, and I had Rs. one lakh fifty thousand in my savings. This meant I needed to save Rs. 12,500 every month.

The financial goal was a foreign vacation with a target amount of three lakhs. The time horizon was 12 months, with Rs. 150,000 coming from my savings account and Rs. 12,500 saved each month for 12 months. Had I not planned our travel in 2011, it could have become an emergency in 2012, forcing me to withdraw Rs. 150,000 from savings and borrow the remaining amount. Planning helped us manage our expenses effectively.

Fortunately, our foreign vacation was just a year later. Most other financial goals are set for ten, fifteen, or even thirty years in the future. Prices will inevitably rise because of inflation. So, saving every month for a goal must account for inflation, meaning the rate of return or interest should exceed inflation. For instance, if inflation is 8% per year, the rate of interest should be higher than 8%.

While many are mentally aware of their financial goals, they often lack clarity on how much they will need when they reach those milestones. This is a common issue for many families. They fail to factor in inflation and do not know how much they should save at what interest rate. For example, many parents are aware of the current fees for undergrad studies but do not account for inflation or save according to the target mentioned above.

Examples: Financial goals and target savings

Below is a table illustrating an example of a young family in their 30s who currently spends Rs. 50,000. If they retire at 60 years, the inflated expenses then would be Rs. 2.90 lakhs. If they expect to live another 30-40 years while maintaining the same lifestyle, with inflation at 5%, they will require a retirement corpus of approximately Rs. 8.20 crores which will earn interest of 7.5% post tax.

Assuming they receive retirement benefits from their company and provident fund totalling Rs. 1 crore, they will need to generate the remaining Rs. 7.20 crores through savings. If the family invests Rs. 23,000 every month at a 12% rate of return, they can easily generate that corpus.

Retirement goal	
Current age (years)	30
Retirement age (years)	60
Life expectancy (years)	100
Current inflation in 2024	6%
Expenses per month (current)	50,000
Expenses per month (1st year of retirement)	2,90,000
Corpus required on retirement day	8,20,00,000
Retirement benefits projected	1,00,00,000
Remainder to be generated through savings/investments	7,20,00,000
Rate of return expected from current investments	12%
Savings per month starting today	23,000
Inflation during retirement years (30 years later)	5%
Rate of return-post tax(during retirement)	7.50%

Retirement goal projection

Another example involves funding a child's higher education. If a child is currently 1 year old and will need Rs. 20 lakhs in 17 years with an inflation rate of 10%, the fees will rise to around Rs. 1 crore. To reach that target, this family will need to save approximately Rs. 15,000 each month for the next 17 years at a 12% rate of return.

Children's higher studies fees	
Age of child (years)	1
Funds required after # of years	17
Current fees inflation	10%
Current fees (INR)	20,00,000
Fees after # of years (INR)	1,00,00,000
Rate of return on current investments	12%
Savings per month starting today (INR)	15,000

Children's higher studies fees projections

Below is an example of the target corpus and required savings for a family with two children.

Financial goal	Today's cost	Target corpus	# of years later	Savings per month
Retirement	Rs 50,000 pm	8,00,00,000	40	23000
Child 1's education	Rs 20 lakhs	76,00,000	14	17000
Child 2's education	Rs 20 lakhs	1,00,00,000	17	15000
Child 1's wedding exp	Rs 10 lakhs	98,00,000	24	6000
Child 2's wedding exp	Rs 10 lakhs	1,31,00,000	27	5000
				66000

Financial plan for a family of two children

Just imagine if this family had no financial goals or planning. How confident can they be that they will be able to fund all their requirements? Many families are unaware and face setbacks when the time comes for their financial goals. For instance, if this family fails to account for inflation and saves based on the current Rs. 20 lakhs fees, they will panic when it escalates to Rs. 76 lakhs after 14 years for their first child. Had they done proper planning, they would have saved accordingly.

In this example, a family needs to save Rs. 66,000 in addition to their monthly expenses. At the end of this book, I have provided a link to download an Excel file where you can calculate your own financial goals, targets, and savings.

Long-Term Investing

I recall a young man who told me after attending one of my online financial planning sessions during the pandemic:

"I am not comfortable investing. What should I do?"

"What steps do you take with your money now?" I asked.

"I keep my salary in a savings account. It's been accumulating for years," he replied nonchalantly.

"You have lost lakhs to inflation. Withdraw it immediately and invest in a fixed deposit or mutual funds," I told him with an urgency

I couldn't fathom how much he had lost over the years by keeping his money in a savings account, which typically yields an average of 3% interest, while inflation averages over 5%. Ideally, he should have invested in a long-term product that offers returns of 8-10%.

Observing typical financial goals such as retirement, children's education, and marriage, which are 10, 20, or 30 years in the future, it becomes clear that savings alone won't suffice to reach these targets as they cannot outpace inflation. Long-term investments are the only viable option that can yield returns above 8-10%. Equities, bonds (fixed income), gold, and real estate are some options that can provide returns that outstrip inflation. In my 30 years of experience in financial services, I cannot think of a better long-term investment option than equities. However, one should not invest everything in equities; an asset allocation strategy is essential, which I will explain separately below.

Systematic Investment

"Dishonest money dwindles away, but whoever gathers money little by little makes it grow." (Proverbs 13:11). This Bible verse has profoundly impacted my approach to investing. One of the best ways to grow your wealth is through systematic investing. Avoid falling into the trap of get-rich-quick schemes. The only time-tested method is to invest a small sum every month from your income. Warren Buffet built his wealth through regular and consistent investing over the years. The greatest virtue required for wealth accumulation is patience.

In India, mutual funds allow systematic investing through a plan called the Systematic Investment Plan (SIP). Mutual fund managers invest the pooled corpus from investors into the stock market. While they can be volatile in the initial years, they are risky, but over the long term, they have yielded average returns of over 15% in India. Their returns surpass those of fixed deposits, postal savings, or any other bonds, including government bonds.

Although I used to invest in mutual funds, it was only in 2012 that I began SIPs, which transformed my investing journey. I cannot overemphasise the magic of investing through SIPs. This is a proven way to grow wealth when you save consistently each month. It has more to do with human behaviour and psychology than mathematics. You need discipline and a commitment to invest. Coupled with a high rate of return, like in a mutual fund, there is no better way to experience the power of compounding.

I strongly recommend starting a monthly SIP if you haven't already. If you have started, I suggest increasing your SIP every month, known as a step-up SIP. The table will show you the difference between a normal SIP and a step-up SIP.

	Normal SIP	Step up SIP
SIP amount per month	5000	5000
SIP amount per year	60000	60000
% increase in SIP pa	0%	10%
Return on investments	15.00%	15.00%
Period of investments (yrs)	30	30
Future value after the investment period	2,99,97,415	6,72,92,070

Rs. 5,000 per month for 30 years at a 15% return will grow to Rs. 3 crores. However, if you increase your SIP by 10% every year, it will grow to Rs. 6.75 crore, more than double the amount. This is the power of SIP, compounding, and increasing consistently.

Asset Allocation

Real estate and gold are two favourite assets of many in India, while others invest solely in equities. Asset allocation is a simple yet effective strategy that is often underrated. Emotions like greed and fear can influence our investment decisions, whereas principles of asset allocation should guide us. The goal of any investment plan is to increase returns while minimising risk, which is achieved through asset allocation.

Every investment portfolio should consist of a mixed basket of asset classes. An asset class is a type of investment type that has certain unique characteristics. For example, equity is an asset class. Other asset classes include fixed income, cash, real estate, and gold. Among all asset classes, equities are the most rewarding but also carry the highest risk and volatility. In India, equities have provided average returns of 15% and above over the last thirty years. It is advisable to remain invested for at least five years to mitigate volatility.

Therefore, a young family should allocate the largest proportion of their investments to equities, as most financial goals are set far into the future. Retirement may be thirty years away, children's higher education may be fifteen years or more, and children's weddings may be twenty-five years in the future. There is no better asset class than equities. The remainder should be allocated to fixed income, real estate, and gold. Any financial goal with a time horizon of less than five years should be assigned to fixed income. Gold serves as a safe haven during times of national crisis or high inflation, while real estate provides steady income through rents.

Another important aspect of asset allocation is the risk profile. Individuals with a high risk profile can allocate a higher percentage to equities, while those with a low-risk profile should allocate a smaller percentage. A risk profile quantitatively assesses an individual's or entity's ability to withstand risk. It can describe an individual's risk tolerance or the level of risk they are willing to accept. Those new to mutual fund or stock market investing typically have a lower risk profile compared to seasoned investors.

When reaching financial goals, the funds should ideally be shifted from equities to cash. This summarises the concept of asset allocation.

Need for Financial Planning in India

According to an article on financialexpress.com in December 2023, retirement planning has significantly declined in India this year, with the percentage of savings directed toward retirement dropping compared to 2022, as revealed by a recent Bankbazaar survey. Women have been particularly affected, with only 34.3% saving for retirement compared to 48.45% last year. For men, the figure remains relatively stable at 40.1%, down slightly from 41.86% last year.

In a January 2024 article by Morningstar, a study by Max Life Insurance found that nearly half of the participants have not started saving for retirement. Additionally, 61% worry they will run out of retirement savings within ten years, and 90% of Indians aged 50 and older regret not starting to save earlier for retirement.

Conversely, a new study by the Financial Planning Standards Board (FPSB) highlights how professional financial planning has improved the quality of life for Indian consumers. The report also provides insights into the outcomes for retired individuals. According to the study, 80% of Indian consumers feel that professional financial planning services have enhanced their quality of life, and 75% feel more financially confident.

Do you see the importance of financial planning? If you haven't started setting financial goals and saving systematically toward them, I hope you now realise their significance.

We often think tomorrow is a better day to start, but I urge you to begin today. This discipline changed the trajectory of our finances, and I cannot overemphasise its importance.

> **Planning common financial goals is the fifth step in growing your wealth and strengthening your marriage.**

Questions for Discussion:
1. Have you planned your common financial goals and started targeted savings?

2. If you aren't budgeting and tracking expenses, write down what the biggest demotivator is and how budgeting could benefit your finances.

3. Have you started a Systematic Investment Plan (SIP) in mutual funds? If not, when do you plan to start? If yes, note the financial and non-financial benefits you currently enjoy.

* * *

A well-known money and marriage coach stood before a large crowd doing his usual training. He just finished talking about investment plans, mutual funds, and stocks. Just then a hand shot up from the crowd.

"I have a question, sir," a young man stood up. "Thank you, sir, for such a life-transforming training session on managing money. My question is, I am so excited to invest, but the rising costs make it impossible to invest. By the end of the month, there's nothing left," said the man.

The coach paused, locking eyes with him. "That's a great question. To answer that, I have a question for you: How much of your salary goes to pay your EMIs?"

A silence fell over the audience.

"EMI?" said the man with a confused look on his face. "I thought we were focusing on investments today."

"You are right, we are talking about investments now, but do you know that debt or loans is your biggest enemy in growing your wealth?" said the coach.

He continued, "However much you invest, as long as you have debt, it's like taking one step ahead and two steps back. It's like building your house on sand with no strong foundation. Heavy rains and the building collapses."

"My talk would be incomplete without discussing debt, which has mastered so many and even killed," said the coach.

"How many of you want to hear what is debt and how to get rid?" asked the coach.

All hands went up promptly.

STEP 6– CONQUERING: "MANAGE DEBT"
Step of Avoiding Toxicity

This section contains two chapters. Chapter one covers how debt, like a disease, threatens family financial health. Ignoring it leads to mounting interest and prolonged repayment, harming both present and future stability. Chapter two covers transforming financial stress into financial freedom by managing debt. It shares Café coffee day's debt-reduction journey, practical debt-repayment strategies, budgeting tips, health impacts, marriage dynamics, and the power of replacing debt habits with wealth-building practices for long-term financial and relational stability.

Chapter 9

Master Debt Before Debt Masters

"Debt is like a disease that threatens the financial health of a family. Unless diagnosed early and treated immediately, it can cripple the present and destroy the future."

Sushma picked up her phone in a last desperate attempt to help her parents escape debt. She called the financial advisor her friend recommended. The advisor answered the call.

"I am in deep distress! My parents took loans from friends and family a few years ago. We have repaid a lot of the loan in the last few years, yet today the outstanding loans total Rs. 80 lakhs. I just don't know what to do!" Sushma exclaimed to the advisor.

She continued, "My father is retiring in the next six months, and his retirement money is not even one-third of the debt we owe."

"Why did your parents take on such a huge debt?" the advisor asked.

"They took the loan first for my brother's further studies abroad and then for his marriage. My brother has since repaid most of the loans but has abruptly stopped repaying. He is weary of the mounting interest and doesn't take our calls anymore," Sushma said in a feeble voice over the phone.

Sushma's struggle is part of a much larger issue that affects households globally.

Global household debt

According to an article on marketwatch.com, US household debt reached a record high of $17.3 trillion (Rs. 1,436 lakh crores), while household debt in India currently stands at $671 billion (Rs. 56 lakh crores). Household debt refers to the money individuals borrow, typically from banks or financial institutions, to be repaid in the future. This includes mortgage/home loans, personal loans, student loans, credit card loans, and auto loans.

Based on India's current population, the rough estimate of households should be around 30 crores. The average debt per household amounts to approximately Rs. 2 lakhs. Assuming a family earns an average salary of Rs. 25,000 per month, each family carries a debt equivalent to around 8-10 months of their salary. Clearly, some households may bear significant debt, extending over several years of their salary. Like Sushma's family, many others are drowning in debt.

I know the numbers can be overwhelming and tedious. You don't need to remember them. To put it simply, the loans that families are taking are high and continue to grow.

Instant Gratification Compounds

David and Trisha both had well-paying jobs, which provided ample opportunities for lavish spending soon after their marriage. Instead of capitalising on their substantial disposable income to save or start a SIP, they opted for the instant gratification route of EMIs. The most appealing thing about EMIs was that they allowed them to purchase an expensive car, a large TV, and household items worth lakhs by paying only a small EMI.

One day, David lost his high-paying job during an economic downturn. They suddenly faced the daunting challenge of managing huge EMIs without any emergency funds. Instead of prioritising loan repayment, they decided to pledge their gold and take out another loan.

They expected David to find a new job soon, allowing them to return to their previous lifestyle. However, David struggled to secure suitable employment, and the mounting EMIs began to exert pressure. To alleviate the pressure temporarily, Trisha took out a personal loan. After a year of job searching, David still hadn't found work, prompting them to consult a financial advisor.

Most loans begin small, often for a need or a want. While taking a loan for a necessity may be justifiable, taking one for a desire is not. Unfortunately, accumulating loans can become a much larger problem than the original need for which the loan was taken. They could have likely lived without the loan had they known it would spiral into a debt trap. Most household loans reflect changing values, times, and the importance placed on materialism and instant gratification.

Types of Loans

Not all loans or debts are the same. Just as an ordinary viral fever differs from influenza or COVID-19, some loans are mild while others are serious. Each loan can indicate the severity of your financial situation. In Sushma's case, as well as David and Trisha's, the loans are no ordinary fever.

There are mainly two distinctions: secured and unsecured loans.

Secured Loans

Secured loans are the better option of the two. They are backed by your assets, such as a home, car, gold, shares, or mutual funds. This means that if you cannot repay the loan, the lender can sell the asset to recover the loan amount. Secured loans typically have lower interest rates, resulting in lower EMIs. The repayment period is also longer, and borrowing limits are higher.

Within secured loans, home loans, educational loans, and business loans are considered good loans. Gold loans may also be considered good as long as the funds are used for productive purposes. These loans are deemed good because they are either taken for appreciating assets or are expected to generate better returns in a business or career.

Conversely, car loans and consumer loans are classified as bad loans because their value depreciates over time. As a family, it is best to take good loans rather than bad loans, as good loans can lead to appreciation or higher returns, thereby increasing wealth, while bad loans will ultimately erode it.

Unsecured Loans

Unsecured loans, in my opinion, are undesirable loans often taken for unnecessary desires. Credit card loans and personal loans fall into this category. These loans lack collateral, resulting in high interest rates and shorter durations. For example, credit card loans carry interest rates of 30-40%, while personal loan interest rates vary from 10.50-24%.

These loans are often taken to consolidate or repay debt, address emergencies, fund weddings, make home improvements, or finance vacations. In many cases, personal loans are taken for home construction when housing loans reach their limit. More often than not, the loan repayment lasts for years while the benefits of the loan are enjoyed in just a matter of days.

Happy Loan Turns Sad

Rohan took a personal loan for his lavish wedding, confident he could repay it from his monthly salary. Five years into his marriage, he is still repaying that loan, which has placed significant strain on their already tight budget. This is a classic example where the repayment period extends for years, while the so-called benefit was experienced in just a day or two days. The same goes with emergencies and vacations.

These loans gradually deplete your wealth, both present and future. Each month, EMIs diminish your capacity to create long-term wealth in exchange for something that could have been avoided. Weddings and emergencies could have been managed effectively in earlier years, preventing the need for loans and avoiding this unprofitable path.

Home loans

Among all loans, home loans are the only type I consider desirable for a family. They typically have the lowest interest rates, and in India, you get tax exemptions, effectively reducing your interest rate further. Property as an asset class appreciates at 6-8% per annum in India, allowing you to build a long-term asset.

That said, as a financial planner, I strongly recommend that young couples avoid taking housing loans until their forties or until they have built a big, growing corpus primarily consisting of equities. In my previous chapter on financial planning, I mentioned compounding and asset allocation.

Baggage from the Past

Many couples enter marriage with baggage, both in terms of possessions and loans, with wedding loans being the most prominent. Many take educational or home loans years before their marriage. I had taken a home loan long before we got married and was paying the EMI for several years into our marriage.

Rohan, in our previous story, never disclosed to his fiancé Irene that he had taken a wedding loan. One day, after they were married, Irene happened to see the bank statement and became curious.

"What is this large payment for? I can't make it out. I don't remember purchasing anything last month for this amount," Irene asked, frowning at the computer screen.

"That's the loan I took for our wedding. You know I don't earn a big salary that would allow me to save and spend on this wedding," Rohan replied.

"You never told me. How big was the loan?" Irene asked, her voice rising.

Often, these loans are intentionally or unintentionally hidden from each other before marriage, only to surface later. Such revelations can create tension and friction in a marriage, not only because the information was hidden but also due to the unexpected repayment burden, which adds stress to an already tight budget.

If such a situation has happened in your family, the best course of action is to forgive and move forward. Work like a team to repay the loan, regardless of who took it or how large it is. Collaborating toward a common goal, especially one that is an undesirable financial burden, can strengthen your marriage and expedite repayment.

Post-Marriage Loans

Once married, the combined income can create a false sense of security, leading couples to believe their repayment capacity has increased, even as they consume goods and services together. This may seem beneficial for consumption and growth on a national level, but it is detrimental to the couple's financial growth, as seen in David and Trisha's story.

Home improvement loans, car loans, home loans, and consumer durable loans are common among young married couples. No one wants to appear primitive or backward, regardless of their financial situation. Peer pressure keeps couples on their toes regarding their home environment.

I remember when my spouse and I got married over 23 years ago; we consciously decided not to buy a TV for various reasons. Everyone who visited us—relatives, friends, and well-wishers—expressed concern about our lack of a TV and encouraged us to purchase one. They felt sorry for us, believing we couldn't afford even a TV. Some even offered to buy one for us.

Just imagine how a young family feels when they lack basic items at home and how others perceive them. Ironically, couples worry about how others will view them, while friends and family are concerned about the couple's well-being. Instead of focusing on relationships and the couple's adjustment in marriage, friends and family fixate on material possessions that are missing from their home.

Young families often overlook the future implications of loans, focusing instead on maintaining a great house, car, and things at home. While essentials like a fridge or a gas stove are necessary, expensive furnishings and large-screen TVs are not, but rather serve as status symbols when financial resources are limited.

Our No-Loan Wedding and Marriage

I am grateful that we did not take out loans for our wedding or for home improvements or stuff at home. I don't say this out of pride, but I genuinely believe it was the best decision we made. We changed the venue of our wedding because I couldn't afford to hold it in Mumbai. I owe this decision to a dear friend and mentor who encouraged me to create a budget for our wedding. For some reason, I had never been inclined to loans or experienced their allure, so I never considered taking one.

We began our married life without the burden of loans. Shortly after marriage, as I mentioned earlier, a friend offered to help us renovate our newly purchased home. Although I didn't have the funds at the time, he kindly completed the woodwork, and we repaid him later for his services.

Lack of Risk Planning

Many couples today take loans for emergencies from time to time. When adequate health insurance is lacking, couples often resort to loans. Other emergencies, such as sudden travel for family matters, home repairs, vehicle repairs, and other emergencies. Lack of emergency funds (as discussed in the previous chapter) and inadequate health insurance can result in avoidable loans.

Debt is like a disease—one that can control your life. It multiplies quickly and can cripple a family. As long as it exists, it has the potential to cause significant harm. The only remedy is to eliminate it to survive.

Chapter 10

Kill debt and Stay Alive

"Show urgency in getting rid of debt just like how
you got rid of corona virus"

On July 29, 2019, V.G. Siddhartha, founder of the iconic Café Coffee Day, tragically took his own life, overwhelmed by a staggering debt of Rs. 7,200 crore. His note blamed lenders, partners, and tax officials for the immense pressure that led to this devastating decision. Many assumed the brand would collapse with him. However, his wife, Malavika Hegde, refused to let that happen.

Taking over a failing company burdened by enormous debt, she made bold moves to save it. Through sheer determination, by March 2020, she had reduced the debt to ₹3,100 crore, and as of March 2024, it stands at just Rs. 1,363 crore—a remarkable 81% reduction in five years, all without special favours from lenders.

Her resilience transformed Café Coffee Day's fate, demonstrating that even the heaviest debt can be overcome with grit and unwavering resolve. Debt can suffocate and even destroy, but with the right mindset, it can also be conquered. In this chapter, let's explore how you too can eliminate debt and reclaim your financial life.

Confront Debt Boldly

Debt the families accumulate becomes a cumbersome burden that cannot be easily discarded. Families must learn to live with it and gradually reduce it until it becomes manageable and ultimately repaid.

The first step every young couple should take is to assess all their loans. If you are reading this and have already accumulated debt that feels overwhelming, you should do this. Make a list of all your loans, including the amounts and interest rates. This is indeed the first step to stopping this growing monster. If you don't take this step, you will continue accumulating more debt, which will snowball, and you will spend your life fighting this debt for survival. No meaningful wealth will be built.

Take control instead of being controlled

Once you take control, debt will no longer control you. You must become stronger and take decisive steps to regain control. Start with budgeting. List all your expenses and identify unnecessary expenditures that you can cut. Reducing your spending is a significant step in reversing the long-term effects of debt. After trimming unnecessary expenses, create a new budget that is lean and free of waste. Review your variable expenses as discussed in earlier chapters and prune them. Internet, mobile, groceries, travel, and electricity are examples of variable expenses.

Debt Snowball Method

The second step is to repay debt using the snowball method. This is one approach to debt repayment; you can explore other ways too.

List all your debts from smallest to largest. Regardless of the interest rate, focus on repaying the smallest debt first. By reducing your expenses, you will now have some extra money. Save the extra amount and use it to repay the next smallest debt. Once you pay off the first debt, that EMI becomes disposable income. You now have two additional sources of cash: by reducing your spending and repaying the debt. Save this extra cash and target the smallest debt.

For example, if you have four loans totalling Rs. 20 lakhs, Rs. 5 lakhs, Rs. 1 lakh, and Rs. 50,000, focus on repaying the Rs. 50,000 loan first. Let's assume you were paying an EMI of Rs. 5,000, which now becomes your disposable income. In addition, you brought down your expenses by Rs. 5,000. Now you have an extra Rs. 10,000.

Outstanding loans	EMI	Repaying order
50,000	5,000	1
1,00,000	10,000	2
5,00,000	30,000	3
20,00,000	35,000	4
26,50,000	**80,000**	

Loan repayment sequence

Your first temptation will be to spend or take out another loan. But remember, you are reversing the trend. Just like overcoming addiction, you have to put forth your best effort to repay the debt. With the additional Rs. 10,000 saved for ten months, you can then repay the Rs. 1 lakh loan. Assuming your EMI was Rs. 10,000, you now have an additional Rs. 20,000 (Rs. 5,000 + Rs. 5,000 + Rs. 10,000). If you receive a bonus, your first priority should be to repay the debt, not to buy new things. Remember, you are reversing the trend. You are doing the opposite of what you used to do. By taking loans, you were moving backward; now you are reversing those steps and moving forward.

By sincerely following this strategy, you can repay all your loans within a few years. Assuming you had an EMI of Rs. 80,000 per month, all that money will now be yours, not for spending or taking out a new loan but for investing and compounding.

Debt: A Leak in Your Wealth

Debt works like negative compounding on your wealth, so any positive compounding benefits from investing are negated quickly, giving a false sense of wealth creation

Debt is the antithesis of growing wealth exponentially through compounding. When you invest, your money grows through compounding. When you take loans for depreciating assets and repay them through EMIs, it is the opposite of wealth accumulation. In fact, it is a gradual theft of your wealth, which would otherwise grow exponentially. It is the reversal of compounding.

Debt is akin to trying to run with a heavy load. Even Usain Bolt, the fastest man on earth, would struggle to run quickly with a heavy burden on his shoulders. The same applies to our finances. We may attempt to save and invest our wealth for high returns, but the repayment of loans significantly slows our growth. The only solution is to lighten the load. Repay the loans, and then your investments will grow.

Consider the figure below, which illustrates two households: one with only investments and the other with investments plus loans. In the first 10-15 years the gap isn't substantial, but as time progresses, the compounding effect kicks in, and the gap widens. Although both households started with the same amount (Rs. 1 lakh), after 30 years the household with loans has a retirement corpus of Rs. 3 crores, while the household without loans has a retirement corpus of Rs. 15 crores. The Rs. 12 crore gap is a result of interest paid and the inability to grow wealth through compounding.

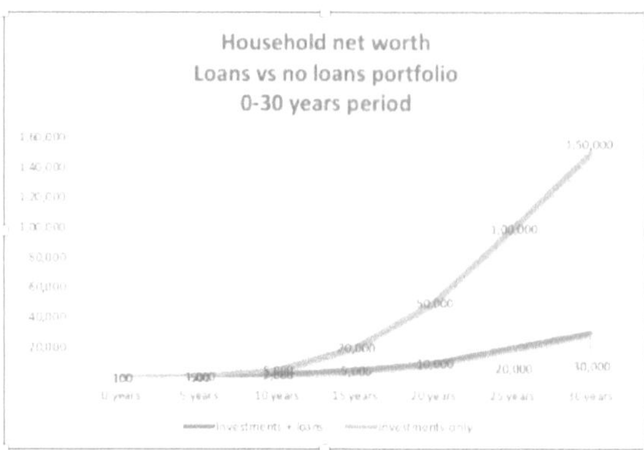

Two households: Investments vis-a-vis Investments plus loans

Note: This is merely a representation chart to illustrate the disparity.

Stress and Health

Mahesh lost his job and struggled to find a new one for an extended period. As the sole breadwinner, he attempted to start a business and took out a loan while also starting day trading in the stock market to generate quick profits. Unfortunately, his business failed, and he incurred losses from the stock market. He continued his job search.

To make ends meet, Sneha his wife tried for a job and fortunately secured a well-paying job. However, the job was stressful, and repaying the debt became her prime goal. Later that year, during her regular health check-up, she discovered she had developed diabetes and high blood pressure.

Constantly living with debt can lead to physical, emotional, and mental health issues. Families burdened by debt often worry about meeting their EMI payments on time, managing their next purchases, or covering school fees. These are real anxieties that can cripple one's mental well-being and bring stress.

Stress from debt can adversely affect physical health in various ways. Constantly living on stress can lead to high blood pressure, negatively impact heart health, weaken the immune system, and cause insomnia. Debt is closely linked to mental health challenges. Individuals with debt are more likely to experience prolonged stress, depression, and anxiety. Couples may also feel guilty and ashamed of their debt.

Stress in Marriage

There is little doubt that debt can adversely impact a marriage. One of the biggest stressors and sources of conflict is financial problems. In smartcouples.ifas.ufl.edu, this is what the article states.

A study involving more than 4,500 married couples revealed that those who took on more debt over time were more likely to separate. Couples with higher debt levels also reported more frequent arguments about money and lower marital satisfaction.

In a second study focusing on newlyweds, researchers found that taking on credit card debt was associated with decreased marital satisfaction. Conversely, paying off debt correlated with increased satisfaction. When new couples incurred debt, they tended to argue more, spend less time together, and perceive unfairness in how finances were managed within their marriage.

According to a Couples & Money study by Fidelity, over half of all couples in the U.S. enter their relationships with debt, and 40 percent report that this financial burden negatively affects their relationship.

Good habits and financial freedom

James Clear, in his book Atomic Habits, writes:

> It's hard to change your habits if you never change the underlying beliefs that led to your past behaviour. You have a new goal and a new plan, but you haven't changed who you are. Habits are like the atoms of our lives.

To achieve financial freedom early in life, simply repaying loans is not enough; that is just the beginning. Developing a habit of avoiding loans while actively saving and investing is crucial. Together, these practices will help you reach your financial goals and ultimately attain financial independence. Without a proactive plan for saving, you may find yourself taking on loans again.

"Old habits die hard," so to overcome a bad habit, you must actively replace it with a good one. Revisit your financial goals and recognise that while you were busy paying EMIs and repaying loans, you were likely unable to invest. Now, with more disposable income, you can embark on your wealth-building journey. This can only happen if you remain disciplined and proactive in setting aside money for investment.

Ketan and Disha's story is a testament to redemption after years of struggling with multiple loans. They felt hopeless about ever being able to invest. However, they made a bold decision to consult a financial advisor, which marked the turning point in their lives. Their advisor helped them create a loan repayment plan, build an emergency fund, and initiate a Systematic Investment Plan (SIP). They eventually paid off their bad loans and are now on the path to growing their wealth.

This simple habit of saving and investing regularly can be a game changer for you and your family. In the coming years, your wealth will grow exponentially due to the power of compounding. This will likely be one of the biggest tests of your life: relinquishing a bad habit and cultivating a good one. This change will alter the trajectory of your life.

You will turn your financial well-being upside down. From being a debtor and feeling financially constrained, you can embark on your journey toward financial freedom.

> Managing debt is the sixth step on your path to building wealth and nurturing your marriage together.

Questions for Discussion:
1. If you have outstanding loans, can you work out a repayment plan together? Write down the dates by which you will repay them.

2. List the reasons why you ended up taking loans. Was there a way to avoid this?

3. Are you currently experiencing conflicts right now

because of debt in your family? What do you think would help resolve these conflicts?

* * *

Finally, after months of relentless rain and humidity, the sun cast its warmth over the city. The streets were alive again with the familiar hustle and bustle of traffic. Inside the car, light instrumental music played softly. Dev was at the wheel, humming along to a tune, while Arya, his wife, gazed out of the window, seemingly lost in thought. Every now and then, Dev glanced at her. In the back seat, their daughter Anusha smiled occasionally as she peeked into the bag of clothes and shoes they'd just bought from the mall.

As a family, they had come a long way. The quietness in the car now was a stark contrast to the storm they had weathered for the past five years, fighting their way out of debt. They had followed every step diligently, and today, they were finally debt-free.

As they drove down a familiar street, Arya suddenly turned and stared intently at something outside. "Stop the car, Dev," she said urgently.

"What is it?" Dev asked, his face full of concern.

"Just stop," she repeated, already unbuckling her seat belt.

Dev pulled over, both curious and a little anxious.

"Just give me five minutes; I'll be right back," Arya said as she opened the door and stepped out, heading toward a small roadside restaurant. Dev and Anusha exchanged puzzled looks.

"Maybe she's buying us something," Anusha suggested, glancing at her dad. "Maybe it's the shawarma I like!"

They watched as Arya disappeared into the open restaurant. A few minutes later, she came out with a bag, but instead of returning to the car, she walked in the opposite direction—toward a woman and a small child sitting by the roadside, their clothes dusty and worn.

Dev and Anusha remained silent as they watched Arya hand them the food. The woman's eyes widened with gratitude, and the child eagerly began opening the packet. Arya exchanged a few words with them, smiled warmly, and then made her way back to the car.

As she got in, Dev looked at her with admiration. "That was so kind of you. I never expected it. No wonder you were looking out the window all this time. You're an angel."

Arya smiled softly as she buckled her seat belt. "We already have more than enough. Remember what the Bible says? 'It is more blessed to give than to receive.'"

Dev thought back to the days when they had little to give, yet Arya always found a way—to help a neighbour in need, give to the church, or offer something to a stranger. No matter how little they had, she never stopped being generous.

Anusha, now understanding, leaned forward and rested her chin on the seat in front of her. "I want to do that too, Ma, when I grow up. I want to give."

Arya smiled at her daughter. "You don't have to wait to grow up, sweetie. You can start now. God has blessed you with so much. You can begin today."

Anusha looked at her bag of new clothes and shoes and smiled, as if she had just found her own mission.

STEP 7 – GIVING: "GROW YOUR GENEROSITY INDEX"

Step of Building Joy and True Freedom of the Soul

This section contains two chapters. Chapter one covers the profound impact of generosity, highlighting its power to bring joy, strengthen relationships, reduce materialism, and foster fulfilment through blessings that transcend mere financial gain. Chapter two covers the journey of generosity, showing how a giving spirit can create a legacy. Through stories like Colgate and Tata, it urges families to cultivate generosity, creating meaningful societal impact for future generations.

Chapter 11
Generosity Index's bull run

"Generosity is a blessing that is truly experienced only after the act of giving. The joy of giving cannot be adequately described by the giver, nor can the blessings be measured."

"**W**ere we to use more than 1% of my claim checks on ourselves, neither our happiness nor our well-being would be enhanced. In contrast, that remaining 99% can have a huge effect on the health and welfare of others."

These words belong to Warren Buffet, the greatest investor the world has ever known. In 2006, he made the Giving Pledge, committing to donate 99% of his wealth to philanthropy during his lifetime or at his death. This quote is an excerpt from that pledge. He is not only the greatest investor but has also become one of the most significant philanthropists, having donated $46.1 billion so far, according to Forbes.com. He has raised the bar for generosity, effectively raising the generosity index for himself and his family.

Generosity and Index

In the previous chapters, I focused on how to build your wealth—first by spending less and then by increasing your returns. In the following pages, I will discuss the opposite: the importance of giving and being generous. As a couple, consider how you can increase your generosity index.

How do you define generosity? According to Webster's dictionary, generosity is "the quality of being generous; liberality in principle; a disposition to give liberally or to bestow favours; a quality of the heart or mind opposed to meanness or parsimony."

To simplify this definition, generosity can be described as "the act of being kind and giving freely." It involves having an open heart and mind, willing to help or share with others without being stingy or selfish.

In one sentence, generosity is when someone gives a lot.

What is an index? An index has several meanings and interpretations, but let me stick to our context: "it is a sign or measure of something."

I have combined these two concepts to create what I call the Generosity Index: a measure or indicator of how much a person, family, or group gives in relation to their capacity. It reflects how willing and consistent someone is in sharing their time, money, or resources with others. The higher the index, the more generous someone is, demonstrating their tendency to give without expecting anything in return. This index can be used to measure generosity in financial contributions, acts of kindness, or any form of giving.

Need for This Chapter

You might wonder if this chapter is truly necessary. Everyone gives at some point, sometimes more and sometimes less. Why dedicate an entire chapter to this topic? Can raising your generosity index lead to financial freedom or a successful marriage? The chances may seem slim, but you would be mistaken if you thought so!

The benefits of being generous and increasing your generosity index extend far beyond what meets the eye. If we could accurately measure the impact of generosity on our lives and relationships, everyone would give freely. So why didn't I include this chapter earlier? Because this is where it fits best. Let me explain.

You cannot give generously if you do not have. To increase your generosity index, you must first grow your wealth. I do not mean to imply that those who have less are not generous. What I mean is that to give generously and continually increase your generosity index, you must cultivate your wealth. Generosity then becomes a joy because you have enough and more.

Generosity is immeasurable

Is generosity easy and natural? Absolutely not! Giving is not instinctive. It is easier said than done. Even an innocent child may be reluctant to share their toys. As we grow older, giving often requires encouragement and reminders. Most of us need strong motivation to give.

For example, spending provides immediate gratification through products or services. Saving or investing offers hope for future growth, as evidenced by investment statements. While spending and investing can be measured, how to measure giving? The first impression is that giving means losing something from our hands or pockets forever, even if we receive a receipt. So how can we be convinced to give and become generous? There are numerous compelling reasons to give, some of which are beyond measure.

Health Benefits

Several studies indicate that generosity improves physical and psychological health. According to www.theconversa tion.com a study involving 128 older adults showed that generosity lowers blood pressure. Previously diagnosed with high blood pressure, these individuals experienced benefits comparable to those gained from medication and exercise. Other studies also suggest that it reduces the risk of dementia, anxiety, and depression and reduces heart-related problems.

Generosity encompasses more than just monetary contributions; it means a lot. For example, if you are earning Rs. 50,000 per month and you give someone Rs. 50, That hardly matters because you don't feel you could have purchased anything significant. But if you had to help someone with Rs. 1000, now that means a lot to you. You could have purchased part of your groceries, eaten out, and spent on petrol, but you gave because of a need that was bigger than your purchases.

Generosity not just means money but also includes giving time. Time is precious, and sparing for someone who cannot reciprocate is a significant act of generosity. This type of giving offers similar health benefits as financial contributions.

Generosity Keeps You Happy

Generosity contributes to happiness. Happiness arises from the release of chemicals in the brain, such as endorphins, dopamine, and oxytocin. For instance, oxytocin, known as the "love hormone," is released when you fall in love or feel loved, creating happiness. Dopamine is released when you achieve something, experience pleasure, or engage in activities you enjoy. Endorphins are similar hormones that alleviate pain and enhance happiness. Studies show that generosity triggers these feel-good hormones in our brains.

In their book "The Paradox of Generosity," sociologists Christian Smith and Hilary Davidson present findings from the Science of Generosity Initiative at Notre Dame. Researchers surveyed 2,000 individuals over five years, tracking the spending habits and lifestyles of 40 families from various backgrounds across 12 states, even accompanying some to the grocery store. The result is one of the most comprehensive studies of Americans' giving habits ever conducted.

According to their study, consistently giving time and money correlates with increased happiness. Their findings also indicate lower depression rates among Americans who donate more than 10 percent of their incomes. Thus, giving has a significant impact on your mental health. Have you ever experienced joy when giving food to someone on the street? That feeling is true happiness, which really cannot be explained.

Strengthens Marriage

Research on generosity and its effects on marriages shows that both the giver and recipient families experience higher levels of marital satisfaction. A study by Fidelity Charitable, conducted among nearly 700 donors, reveals that giving often unites couples. Over 80% of respondents—who were all married or living with a partner—reported that they frequently or always agree with their partner on household giving decisions, such as which charities to support and how much to contribute. Only 11% of donors reported regular disagreements over giving decisions, typically concerning the amount or choice of charities.

According to Fidelity Charitable, giving sparks meaningful conversations that deepen intimacy and strengthen the core of a partnership. Typical marital discussions revolve around earning, spending, and saving. However, giving provides an opportunity for couples to discuss values and purpose, leading to deeper conversations. Elaine Martyn, Vice President of Fidelity Charitable's private donor group, notes that disagreements over charitable giving can be challenging, as it still involves money. However, philanthropy can serve as a positive means of communicating for couples

Builds Virtues

Generous couples who give to those outside their relationship are often generous to each other as well. Ideally, generosity should begin at home, but it does not necessarily happen. However, when couples who are engaged in giving develop empathy, kindness, and compassion. These virtues naturally impact their marriage and loved ones.

All three virtues focus on others rather than oneself. A strong marriage is characterised by individuals who prioritise their partner's needs over their own. A happy marriage is one where both partners feel loved and cared for. Generosity, both outside and within the marriage, embodies selflessness. When both of you are growing in their giving, you are naturally benefiting yourself.

Reduced Spending

Over time, generosity heightens awareness of others' needs, leading to reduced personal spending. It encourages reflection on financial habits and prioritises giving where it is most needed. For instance, during the COVID-19 pandemic, many individuals and NGOs stepped up to distribute food to those in need. This experience often made them more conscious of their spending habits, shifting their focus from personal indulgence to community support.

As you engage in giving, your priorities shift from accumulating material possessions to helping others. This change fosters more mindful spending and reduces impulse buying. Generosity also increases awareness of societal inequalities, cultivating gratitude for what you have and diminishing the urge for unnecessary purchases. Instead, you begin to live more simply and purposefully.

The satisfaction of helping others often brings a deeper sense of fulfilment than material possessions can provide. This reduces the need to seek happiness through spending, leading to more controlled and thoughtful financial decisions.

A study by Harvard Business School (Dunn, Aknin, & Norton, 2008) found that people who spend money on others feel happier than those who spend on themselves. This happiness derived from giving encourages a more conscious approach to spending, as the joy of helping others outweighs the desire for personal possessions.

Another study published in the Journal of Positive Psychology (2013) indicates that generosity reduces materialism and increases life satisfaction, naturally leading to less unnecessary spending.

Fulfilment and Meaning

Generosity is unparalleled and distinct. Spending is instinctive, and saving or investing requires discipline, both of which focus on the future for ourselves, our families, and potentially future generations. However, generosity is fundamentally different. When you give, you selflessly consider the impact on others' lives. There is little for your own gain. What you receive in return is a blessing.

What is the true meaning of a blessing? A blessing is something deeper and cannot be measured materially. The joy, peace, and happiness that accompany giving are indescribable. At various points in our lives, we find that the meaning of life lies not in receiving but in giving. Fulfilment comes not from abundance but from sharing the abundance. No wonder the Bible states, "It is more blessed to give than to receive" (Acts 20:35).

In a community like ours, numerous opportunities exist to find meaning and purpose. Giving and sharing what God has provided you is one of life's greatest purposes. It is akin to sowing a seed, with benefits reaped not just by you but by future generations.

Chapter 12

Generosity a family venture

"The wealthy will always pass on an inheritance to their many generations; it's the generous wealthy who will pass on a legacy too!

On August 1, 1992, I received my first salary of Rs. 1,200. At that moment, I didn't know, but a seed of generosity was being sown. With great humility and gratitude, I want to share my journey of giving. When I received that first salary, I set aside 10% and donated it to the church I attended, thanking God for the teachings I had received. The Bible teaches about tithing, which is giving 10%. By setting aside this amount, I learnt the importance and the blessings of giving. As my salary increased, I started giving to charity and supporting the needy.

Generosity Needs a Start

I was once the recipient of the generosity of two seniors who helped me purchase study materials for the competitive exams I was preparing for. Remember, there was no internet then, so buying books and materials was the only option. Thanks to their kindness, I successfully passed the SBI mutual fund exam and secured a breakthrough in the industry where I have spent three decades of my working life.

Years later, God provided me the opportunity to continue this cycle of generosity. I funded a young man's college fees, who came from a poor family. I still remember the joy of giving and being a blessing to him. I was immensely grateful that I got an opportunity to reciprocate the very thing I had received. The abundant blessings of generosity have compelled me to conclude this book with this lesson.

What about you and your family? You can make a fresh start if you haven't considered this a thought. Generosity is not about great wealth but about having a big heart. Decide in your heart to begin today. Start with a small percentage (1% or 2%) of your salary and commit to giving to charity each month. Trust me, you will experience joy that comes only from giving. I challenge you to increase your giving until you reach the milestone of 10%, and then nothing can stop you—not even yourself. As your salary grows, so will your giving. God will ensure that you and your children will never lack. If you are already giving, I encourage you to increase your generosity index.

Highly Rated Families

A generous family, in my opinion, is one of the most highly rated families. Many do not give, some give, and only a few give generously. This world is in need. Many in our country are not as privileged as you and I. They don't even have basic food and shelter, let alone access to schools. If you are reading this book, it means you can afford it. Most likely, you live in a decent home, own a mobile phone, perhaps a laptop, and occasionally take an auto, Uber, or Ola, ride a train, or fly. You dine out or order from Swiggy or Zomato; go on vacations.

Unless those who possess wealth generously give to those who do not, this world will not become a better place to live. Families that care enough and have a plan to give are blessed families. I consider such families to be top-rated families, and I believe God will reward them. This is one of the best things that can happen to a family where everyone learns to give. When a husband, wife, and children all participate in giving, you are among the few top families who contribute. I would call you a highly rated family.

Generations of Generosity

Many stories of generosity have been passed down through generations. Out of the hundreds of such stories, two stand out and inspire me to create wealth while also passing on this value to your next generations.

Bright Colgate

William Colgate was born in January 1783. In 1804, at the age of 21, he decided to pursue a career in soap and candle making. He began working as an apprentice for a soap boiler in New York City. Colgate learnt the trade and saved enough money to start his own business in 1806, founding William Colgate & Company, which focused on manufacturing soap, starch, and candles.

Colgate was a man of deep Christian faith who believed that God was the true owner of his wealth. Early in his career, he vowed to give 10% (a tithe) of his income to the church and charitable causes. As his business prospered, Colgate increased his giving over time, eventually donating 50% of his income to support various charities, educational institutions, and missionary work.

Colgate-Palmolive, continuing the legacy of its founder, William Colgate, is deeply committed to corporate social responsibility and generosity through various global initiatives. The company focuses on improving communities through health, education, sustainability, and disaster relief efforts.

Bright Smiles, Bright Futures® Program: This is one of Colgate's flagship initiatives, aimed at providing free dental screenings and oral health education to children in need.

Sustainability and Environmental Efforts: Colgate is committed to reducing its environmental footprint. The company works toward sustainability goals such as achieving zero waste in manufacturing facilities, reducing water usage, and creating recyclable packaging.

Colgate Cares Foundation: Through this foundation, Colgate supports various causes, including disaster relief, health initiatives, and community development.

Employee Volunteerism: Colgate encourages its employees to volunteer their time and skills through programs like "Colgate Cares Day," where employees worldwide participate in community service projects.

Water Conservation Initiatives: Colgate promotes water conservation through campaigns such as "Save Water," which encourages people to conserve water while brushing their teeth.

Now let's look at a story closer to home, which brings me immense joy to write about, especially as we fondly remember Ratan Tata, who passed away on October 9, 2024.

Shining Tatas

The Tata Group, one of India's largest conglomerates, exemplifies how generosity can be passed through generations. Founded by Jamsetji Tata in 1868, the company has prioritised social responsibility and community giving.

Jamsetji, known as the "Father of Indian Industry," believed that a company's success should benefit the society that nurtures it. His vision encompassed nation-building and enhancing the quality of life for ordinary Indians.

He established enduring institutions like the Indian Institute of Science (IISc), emphasising education and research, as well as the Tata Institute of Social Sciences (TISS), which continue to focus on healthcare and education.

His son, Sir Dorabji Tata, expanded the family's philanthropic efforts by founding the Tata Trusts in 1919, dedicating two-thirds of the family's wealth to social causes. Notable contributions during his leadership included sponsorship of the Indian Olympic Team in 1924 and support for famine relief and scientific research.

J.R.D. Tata, who led the Tata Group for decades, deepened the legacy of generosity by focusing on creating wealth for societal welfare. He established numerous hospitals, including the Tata Memorial Centre for cancer treatment, and introduced merit-based scholarships while supporting cultural institutions like the National Centre for Performing Arts (NCPA).

Ratan Tata continued this charitable ethos, expanding the group's focus on rural development, healthcare, and education. His notable initiatives include launching the affordable Tata Nano car and the Tata Trusts' substantial contributions during the COVID-19 pandemic, pledging over ₹1,500 crores (approximately $200 million) for medical supplies and vaccine distribution.

This generation will miss Ratan Tata dearly for his contributions to India's economy and philanthropy, but let's not forget that he carried on a legacy of generosity initiated by his great-grandfather.

Passing on Your Legacy

A legacy holds far greater value than an inheritance, as you can see from these two family stories. If you follow the six steps outlined in this book, you are guaranteed to leave an inheritance similar to that of the Colgates and Tatas. It is impossible not to, as these steps contain time-tested principles. However, if you embrace this seventh and final step, you are bound to leave a legacy that can be passed down through generations.

We all want the best for our children in terms of education, clothing, career, and marriage. All these can be provided through material wealth, but there are some, far more important things, which cannot be given through material means, are passed on through spiritual wealth, our character, and inner life. Generosity is one of those invaluable traits.

Generosity is more often caught than taught. Regardless of how great your wealth may be, you cannot teach generosity; it has to be modeled. Our children are often our best imitators in life, even after we are gone. As you grow your generosity index, your relationships will strengthen, you will be blessed, and your future generations will also be blessed, becoming a blessing to society and the nation.

Increasing your generosity index is the seventh and final step to building wealth and your marriage together.

Questions for Discussion:
1. Make a list of people or organisations (including churches, religious institutions, NGOs, etc.) to whom you give. Do you think you can increase your giving?

2. On a scale of 1-5, how would you rate your generosity index (1 being low, 5 being high)?

3. What do you think you need to do as a couple to increase your generosity index? List all your plans and decisions.

Seven Steps to avoid financial mis-steps

C hris and Anna, now in their late thirties, sat at the dining table, worry etched across their faces. Unpaid bills lay scattered around, untouched, and the weight of their mounting debt felt heavier with each passing day. The frustration and stress were written all over their faces as they wondered how to move forward.

Both devout believers were overwhelmed by their situation. Kneeling right at the table, they began to pray. "God, we need help," they pleaded, tears streaming down their faces. "We don't know how to get out of this debt. Please guide us or send us some money.

As their eyes remained closed, they felt a sudden warmth and brightness, as if a glow had fallen upon their faces. When they opened their eyes, they gasped in shock. Before them stood an angel. Chris and Anna, eyes wide with awe, momentarily forgot their worries in the divine presence.

"Fear not," the angel said with a gentle smile. "I bring good news and something God has asked me to give you." The couple held their breath, expecting a miracle of money—cash or gold, perhaps. The angel handed them a packet. Eagerly, they tore it open but were met with disappointment. It was a book.

"But we were hoping for money," Chris said hesitantly.

"God knows what is best for you," the angel replied. "What you need isn't money, but the skills to manage it well."

The angel continued, "This book contains seven steps to transform your financial situation. Follow them, and you'll regain control and find peace in your finances."

Accepting this as God's will, they took the book, their hearts filling with hope. The angel began to outline the steps:

"**Step 1: Combine your finances**. Think of it as 'ours,' not 'mine' and 'yours.' Open a joint account and combine your money. Unity in your finances will foster unity in your relationship. This step lays the foundation for a strong marriage and helps grow your wealth."

"**Step 2: Communicate and be transparent**. Share your financial thoughts and feelings openly. Don't hide anything. Transparency is essential for a healthy partnership. This step requires trust and courage."

"**Step 3: Understand each other's money personalities**. Knowing how each of you views money will help you navigate decisions together. You'll appreciate each other's perspectives and avoid judgment. This step fosters self-awareness and understanding."

"**Step 4: Create a risk plan.** Begin executing your overall financial plan, starting with a 'Risk Plan' that includes term insurance, health insurance, and an emergency fund. This protects your wealth from uncertainties. This step is all about mitigating risks."

"**Step 5: Write your financial goals**. A shared vision will motivate you both. Outline your spending and investment plans together. Write down your financial goals and start budgeting. Invest for the long term to meet goals like retirement and children's education. This step leads to financial freedom."

"**Step 6: Manage your debt**. Debt can drain your wealth and strain your relationship. Tackle it strategically. Prioritise what needs immediate attention and develop a plan to overcome it. Leave behind old habits and start fresh. This step will bring you out of toxicity in your life."

"**Step 7: Increase your generosity index**. Remember, 'it is more blessed to give than to receive.' True freedom is found in giving generously from what God has blessed you with. Generosity opens your heart and can positively impact your finances. Seek ways to be more generous and pass on these values to future generations. This step will offer you the true freedom of the soul."

Chris and Anna stood in stunned silence, absorbing every word. Their shock was now mixed with eager anticipation and hope for overcoming their dire situation.

They looked at each other, feeling a renewed sense of confidence. "This is the help we've been waiting for," Chris whispered, his voice full of belief.

"Remember," the angel said, "the journey to financial harmony begins with these steps. But it will require commitment and faith to follow through."

The angel paused, then continued with a challenge: "Before I go, I ask you: Will you take the leap? Will you not only read the book but actively implement these steps, trusting in God and each other?"

"Your journey to financial freedom and harmony begins now."

With a wave of his hand, the angel began to fade, leaving behind the book and a renewed sense of purpose in the couple's hearts.

As the bright light in the room dimmed, Chris and Anna held hands, hugging each other as tears rolled down their faces. Suddenly, Anna pulled away, as though remembering something important.

"Wait, what's the title of this book?" She asked, but the angel was already gone.

Chris chuckled, looking into her eyes with a loving smile. "Does it matter? As long as we're in harmony and making money, we'll be alright."

Anna's eyes lit up. "That's it! That's the title—'Harmony Money!'"

Chris grinned. "No, I think 'Money Harmony' sounds better."

"No, I like 'Harmony and Money,' and that's final!" Anna declared playfully, her tone childlike.

Chris relented with a sly smile. "Alright, alright. Let's make harmony first, then we'll make money."

Laughing together, they both said in unison, "Harmony and Money" their burdens lifted, and their future suddenly looked much brighter.

Final Thoughts

I hope you both liked reading this book and the contents were helpful. I appreciate you taking time to read the book. I hope you can apply the principles and steps mentioned in this book and enrich your marriage and build wealth and leave a legacy of love and generosity.

I would be happy to hear from you! Please share your honest review on amazon or any other online book store from where you purchased the book.

Social media presence

connect@frankyfernandes.com (email)
www.frankyfernandes.com (website)
https://www.youtube.com/@Frankynfernandes
https://www.facebook.com/franky.fernandes.587
https://www.linkedin.com/in/frankynfernandes/
https://www.instagram.com/frankynfernandes/

Financial goals calculator

Attached below is the excel calculator to compute your financial goals target savings and corpus. Download it and use it. To know more about how to use the tool watch my YouTube video: COMMON FINANCIAL GOALS

https://docs.google.com/spreadsheets/d/1vNdkWDFtH P_OZZdt76RbTbrAlJ96kUoWkn6LoTefeGA/edit?gid=82486 5121#gid=824865121

REFERENCES

1. Jenny G Olson , Scott Rick , Deborah research on newly weds and couples married for over 15 years

2. The Ascent – Motley Fool service and Dave Ramsey research conducted on millionaires

3. Gina Grippo-Martinez wealth advisor at Aline Wealth

4. Answers to marriage : Bruce and Carol Britten

5. www.policygenius.com online insurance market place survey

6. Study by American institute of CPAs

7. Article in Indiatimes.com on Covid 19 hospitalisation

8. Article published in India Today

9. Berkshire Hathaway 2001 annual report

10. Article in The Times of India on a survey conducted

by Finology ventures

11. Story of weight loss transformation in Times of India

12. National weight control registry stories

13. Psychology of Money by Morgan Housel

14. The Bible: Proverbs 13:11

15. Article on financialexpress.com on a bankbazaar survey on decline in retirement planning

16. Article by morning star on a study by Max Life Insurance

17. Study by the Financial Planning Standards Board

18. Article on marketwatch.com on global household debt

19. Tragic story of V.G. Siddhartha founder of Café Coffee Day

20. Article in smartcouples.ifas.ufl.edu on a study involving 4500 couples

21. Couples & Money study by Fidelity

22. Warren Buffet's pledge in 2006

23. www.theconversation.com on a study involving 128 older adults

24. "The Paradox of Generosity" book by socialogists

Smith and Davidson

25. Study by Fidelity Charitable conducted among 700 donors

26. A study by Harvard Business School (Dunn, Aknin & Norton, 2008) on spending money on others

27. Study published in Journal of positive psychology (2013)

28. Story of William Colgate and contribution to society

29. Story of the Tatas and their contribution to society

www.ingramcontent.com/pod-product-compliance
Lightning Source LLC
Chambersburg PA
CBHW031407150726
47989CB00002B/567